What Decides Land Prices?

May 14 '08

[illegible]

What Decides Land Prices?

Trends of Japan's Real Estate Market

Akiyoshi Inoue

VANTAGE PRESS
New York

FIRST EDITION

Published by Vantage Press, Inc.
419 Park Ave. South, New York, NY 10016

Manufactured in the United States of America
ISBN: 978-0-533-15792-1

Library of Congress Catalog Card No.: 2007903090

0 9 8 7 6 5 4 3 2 1

Contents

Preface to the English Language Version

Two years have passed since the Japanese version of my book entitled *What Decides Land Prices?* was published by the newspaper *Asahi.* The price of land is a matter of concern not only for economy, administration, and finance, but for practically all fields of human activities, and perhaps because of that I have received many supportive comments as well as opinions.

During the period of bubble economy I kept insisting that the price of land in Japan would decline by half. Although somewhat spotty depending on location, the same tendency as experienced previously has been repeated the last few years after the bubble.

Lately real estate investments by foreign capital are increasing rapidly. Since the way land is distributed and how land prices are determined are not always the same in Japan as in other countries, and auction markets for bad debt; real properties are also somewhat peculiar in this country, it should be helpful for foreign investors to understand them. I will be happy if this book can be of some assistance.

I would like to add that some of the statistical figures used in this book have been replaced with new ones since two years have elapsed since publication of the Japanese version.

For publishing the English version, I owe a great deal to my partner in the United States, Mr. Donald J. Blake, Sr., and his son, Mr. Donald J. Blake, Jr., of Joseph J. Blake and Associates, Inc., and Mr. Tadao Fujimatsu, Board Chair of TFC Inc. I hereby extend my hearty thanks to them.

I would also like to thank Mr. Toshiro Suzuki, Mr. Jathon

Sapsford, and Ms. Yuka Hayashi for translating, reviewing, and rewriting my book to make this English Language Version possible.

Introduction

From Renters to Owners

I believe Japan's property market, having observed it for years, is in the middle of a major transformation.

To understand this historic change, we need to make a brief visit to the past, to the end of the Edo period. Popular novels of this time of warriors and aristocrats recount how common it was in the major urban centers of Kyoto or Edo—today the city we know as Tokyo—for secret, masked emissaries to dart in and out of gates behind which the Samurai class lived on huge lots hundreds of acres in size. The commoners, most famously in such neighborhoods as Edo's "Shitamachi," lived in cheap and cramped new houses.

This situation, with the wealthy enjoying fabulous spreads while the less fortunate made do in squalor, would remain stable for decades, through the Meiji, Taisho and early Showa periods of Japan's history. But the destruction of World War II would change Japan's urban centers beyond recognition, relentlessly subdividing the stately large properties of Edo, now known as Tokyo. The sprawling properties that once defined the seat of the Shogun are now all but gone, leaving thousands of tiny parcels in their place. The result is that Tokyo, and Japan's other urban centers, are now defined by their tight, crowded conditions. The Japanese are ridiculed around the world as living in "rabbit hutches."

Driving this radical shift were several factors, not least of which was the leveling of wealth, both of incomes and possessions, in the wake of the Second World War, a reflection of Japan's egalitarian policies.

In the past, temples, shrines and feudal lords owned vast estates, and rented out big chunks of these holdings to others. There was little embarrassing about renting, which was deeply ingrained in the nation's economic customs. Landowners rented to building owners, who in turn rented to dwellers. These relationships were strong, with traditional comic monologues telling stories a building owner offers a helping hand to his tenant in dire straits, saying, "Tenants are the same as children to a building owner."

Yet after the war ended, wealthy landlords faced hefty property or inheritance taxes under the new government, and needed to raise money. They sold into a new market for small homes, particularly in suburban areas as the burgeoning populations within the cities drove people to seek new developments within commuting distance. By the mid-1960s, subdivision projects were booming along with the economy. Land prices soared, forcing developers to build ever farther out from urban centers, on lots that grew smaller and smaller. For those who could not afford to live in a house with a lot, developers were ready with suburban condominiums.

It was about that time that Japan fell under the trance of the "Land Myth," characterized by such common refrains as: "Land prices will never go down" or "If you own a piece of land, you will never lose." People became anxious that unless they bought a lot now, they would be priced out as values would certainly keep rising. So, those from the countryside came to the city, they quickly secured a housing loan and bought a home. Payments were a hardship, but it was better than missing out on a chance to own. For the Japanese had come to take it for granted that land should be owned. The vernacular took on a new phrase—"My Home"—referring to a subdivision, apartment or condominium.

A Century of Change in Residential Areas

Something dramatic is happening to residential areas.

First, Japanese are returning from the suburbs to the centers of their huge cities. One big reason seems to be the long slide in property value during the past fifteen years of Japan's lackluster economic performance. Falling urban land values mean that many can afford to buy real estate in central city areas with just a small housing loan. As a result, demand is waning for condominiums and homes in distant suburbs, bringing their prices even lower than those in the city.

Second, the way Japanese look at property is changing. Land has long been considered valuable in Japan, but a quirk in its property market has long been that the buildings depreciate each year. One big reason: If hit by an earthquake, the land endures but the building itself is unusable. So those with the money to do so avoided condominiums or apartments. The thinking was that it was better to own land upon which a house is built rather than share rights to the land with neighbors with condos on the same land. But now, more are moving to buy urban condominiums rather than suburban houses. Buyers are becoming aware that city condominiums are not only more convenient, but more earthquake resistant thanks to advanced architectural technologies. Even those who live in urban detached houses are moving to condominiums in the same areas.

Third, the long slide in property values, and the weak demand in the real estate market, has left many property owners stinging, and they are now less hesitant to rent houses or apartments. As prices keep falling, renting becomes a better strategy, understanding that they can buy a house whenever the time is right. This way of thinking resembles the mentality before the war, before Japan's "land myth" of ever rising property prices.

And fourth, Japan's property market is about to consolidate. A falling population, combined with eroding property values, means residential areas once subdivided into small lots will be re-integrated into larger units. In the days of declining birthrates where fewer than one child is seen per family, it is likely that many will sell properties in the suburbs in favor of lots in the city center.

Needless to say, this doesn't bode well for prices in suburban areas. As more and more compare the prices between the city centers and urban areas, suburban prices will seem to be overpriced, inevitably causing a further decline in suburban property values. Those living in the suburban areas will have to reduce prices ever more sharply to sell their parcels to move back in town, thus depressing suburban prices all the more. Those interested in something outside the city may now be expected to pass over the suburbs and head straight for the countryside. As Japan's population continues to age, it will put a huge burden on pensions, payments from which will invariably decline. The pressures on pensioners will be so great, that even living in the suburbs will be too expensive for many, forcing them to abandon city parcels for life in the countryside where the yen will go further. Meanwhile, an increasing number of rich may start leading a double life; living in the city center during the week, and escaping to a home in the countryside—or abroad—for weekends and holidays. Ultimately, the living environment in the country may become far more amenable for the elderly, driven by a growing disparity in nursing care expenses between the city and the country.

To summarize, the population decrease, the impact on business of an aging society, and the resulting population shifts are likely to have a deep impact on land prices. In the future, population and businesses will concentrate in thriving urban areas like Tokyo, as well as in Osaka and Nagoya. Smaller local areas, especially suburban centers, are likely to find themselves in decline, while the deep countryside could very well thrive.

For more than 100 years now, Japan's properties have been divided into ever smaller parcels. But over the coming 100 years, the trend will reverse itself, with residential lots growing again into big, spacious parcels comparable to those in Europe. Until now, redevelopment has meant constructing condominiums to make effective use of available space for many small dwellings. In the future, development will mean putting together several smaller lots to sell a larger property.

The distinction between urban, suburban and country properties will become less clear. As residential properties in the cities become larger in size, more trees will be planted in the yards, making the cities look more like the suburbs. It will also be difficult to draw a line between the small farms and wooded areas of the suburbs and those of the country. The land once split up for suburban houses and condominiums, soon to fall out of favor, could well be turned into parks, green belts or woods. Japan's topography is varied with mountains and valleys, and it can be developed anew for tourism resorts like Switzerland. Farm products from the country could even be a new export item.

My Resume

At this point, I would like to address those readers wondering: "On what grounds can you talk like that?" I am not making these predictions from wishful thinking or off the top of my head. What I have written so far and what you are going to read are based on twenty-five years of my experience as the head of a real estate appraisal company called "Sanyu System Appraisal."

Let me introduce myself. My family was in Toyota in Aichi Prefecture in central Japan and owned some land. After graduating from Gakushuin University in 1959, I was employed by Nihon Seimei Life Insurance Company. I also had interviews with other companies, such as Mitsui Real Estate Company and Tokyu Real Estate Company. I was accepted by Tokyu, but since I was first informed by Nihon Seimei Life Insurance, I took the job there.

Postwar life insurance companies were having a difficult

time. The bonds they sold were worth little more than the paper they were printed on. The insurance business had been undermined by inflation, and premium holders had little good to say about their insurers, which regularly employed war widows as staff and had them give the hard sell to their relatives. Insurance companies, it goes without saying, did not enjoy good reputations. Many who joined had been told by their family, "It is so difficult to get a job these days. We accept your going to work for an insurance company—on condition that you will not hard sell insurance to us." I didn't know anything about the life insurance business. I didn't know how Nihon Seimei had been ranked in the industry either.

In 1971, I was transferred from the company's Tokyo Finance Department to the Department for Affiliate Business, and from there, I was sent to Nissei Theater, where I was assigned to the Dining—Rental Room Department, which arranged for banquets for corporate customers and the like. People thought I was demoted, but I had a feeling that I was going to be assigned to a sales position. While I was with the finance department. I made it a rule to visit client firms, both old and new, and persuaded them to do business with us. On the other hand, none of my colleagues visited our customers. They did not even know where their offices were and what buildings they were in.

My conduct struck many of my senior colleagues as strange, but there was a board member who appreciated what I was doing. I was more than happy to be sent there.

Nissei Theater was built by Nihon Seimei, but its restaurant, and its rental room business, was not doing well. It is located next to Takarazuka Theater run by the Toho group known for the production of motion pictures. Both the Toho group and Nihon Seimei were built by families rooted in the Mitsui conglomerate, or what was formerly known as a *zaibatsu,* or financial combine. Once, these businesses were very close. But they had fallen into tedious animosity over trifling matters.

Despite such circumstances I dared to visit Toho in the neighboring building and met President Tasuro Matsuoka and Executive Director Masumi Fujimoto. I told them that we were going to offer membership conference rooms at Nissei Theater and asked if they would be the first member since they were our next-door neighbor. The membership was a million yen and I believe a member had to pay an additional annual fee. Taking the opportunity, I asked them to patronize our restaurant in the basement, "Actress," which had an excellent chef, reasonable prices, but few customers.

President Matsuoka made his decision on the spot and signed the contract. To Mr. Matsuoka and Mr. Fujimoto, who was a big figure in Japan's theatrical world, the decision was indeed a small matter. But with this small deal, Toho and Nissei were back on good terms.

The sales work seemed to have suited me. While at the finance department, I did not have to bow to people, but at Nissei, I did not mind bowing to people at all. Having gained confidence in sales work, I changed my job in 1973 to newly started Misawa Home, a home developer. I probably chose Misawa because of my interest in real estate and its related business. If I sound irresponsible when I said "probably," this is only because I had not thought that changing a job was such a big deal.

The founder, Mr. Chiyoharu Misawa, was born on exactly the same day as I was and it made me feel particularly close to him. He is certainly a charismatic leader. At Misawa Home, he let me work as I wished, which prepared me for life as an independent businessman. Misawa did not try to set up local sales companies. Instead they had reputable local companies establish firms in order to alleviate their financial responsibilities and to take advantage of their names in selling houses. Later I will talk about the "Entrusted Real Estate Appraisers System," which created some sensations among real estate appraisers, but I got the idea of the system from the Misawa method as well as from the system of using local doctors for examining subscribers' health conditions practiced by life insurance companies.

Starting a New Business at the Age of 42

After working for seven years at Misawa, I started a new company called "Sanyu System Housing Loan." It was in May 1980 and I was forty-two years old. The business that I entered in the commercial registration was "real estate appraisal and investigation and loaning on real estate." As I wrote before, in the middle of the 1960s, more and more people from local areas wanted to own a house and this spawned a boom in developing subdivisions and housing projects. The number of private housing loans by various financial organizations was on the increase. In order to extend a loan, an appraisal of the collateral value of the property is indispensable. Thus new demand for real estate appraisal was being created by financiers. Until then, real estate appraisal had not been conducted unless it was for large-scale investments like public sites or factories. The system was not fit for private housing loans. So, I limited our clients only to financial organizations and by means of such innovated systems as "efficient appraisal documents" and "entrusted appraisers system," we were able to meet their needs and expand our business. Luckily, Sanyu System has been able to keep the top position among our rivals in terms of the number of requests received from financial institutions.

What is written in this book is based on my experience, but the data on which my analysis is based also owes to accumulated data and investigation by Sanyu System and Sanyu System Real Estate Finance Institute.

I named our company "Sanyu," meaning "three friends," after consulting with a fortune teller who suggested that I use the number "3" as it brings in fortune. He reminded me of such well-known company names as "Mitsui," "Mitsubishi," and

"Mitsukoshi" all of which begins with the number 3. So, I am convinced of the power of the number 3, but since I could not use such big names as Mitsui or Mitsubishi, I took the least popular name, "Sanyu." Then later, my old-time friend who was a man of learning asked me if I named the company after words from *Rongo,* written by Confucius. He was kind enough to buy me the book of *Rongo.* I read the book and was greatly impressed. Confucius said, "There are three types of friends who you gain from and three types of friends who you lose from. Make those who are supple and honest your friends. Make those who are sincere your friends and make those who are blessed with knowledge your friends. You will benefit from them. If you make those who are showy, those who are affable but not sincere, or those who are fast talkers your friends, you will not benefit but lose."

The reason that I added "System" is that I wanted to systematize our business not by doing everything by ourselves but through cooperating with others. Adding "Housing Loan" to the company name is because I had wanted to engage in financing for housing. However, I gave it up because the housing loan business as a whole was not doing well. On the occasion of our twentieth anniversary, we changed the company name to "Sanyu System Appraisal." Using the word "appraisal" for the company name, I thought we could even get into the business of appraising jewelry by changing our articles of association without changing the company name.

How is This Book Composed?

I often think of late that my views and thinking are different from those of other people on many things including, of course, land prices. Perhaps because of that, when I talk with my friends, they often look puzzled. So, I thought it prudent and helpful to write my thoughts down, so that I might be as clear as possible about my unusual perceptions. In 2004, I began to put that into practice and it eventually led to writing this book.

This book consists of seven chapters.

The first chapter, "The Continued Slide in Land Prices," analyzes the mechanism of rising land prices brought about by a recent trend of short-term and intensive real estate investments targeted at such properties as those owned by the former national railway company. I predict that such investments cause the prices of adjacent land to fall sharply and overall land prices will drop to a half of current prices in five years.

The second chapter, "Who Will Suffer Because of Lower Land Values?" examines what influence the price fall of land exerts on financial institutions and questions the validity of conventional system of loaning on land. It also considers what problems are involved in project finance and real state investment trusts that attract attention these days.

The third chapter, "Banks and Appraisers during the Bubble Era," depicts the tragedy as a result of cozy relationships between real estate appraisers and financial institutions.

The fourth chapter, "How the Price of Land is Determined," explains how such public prices as posted prices of land or such private prices as those for actual transaction and standardized appraisal and investigation prices are decided.

The fifth chapter, "Who are Real Estate Appraisers?" explains, as the title indicates, what the real estate appraiser does.

The sixth chapter, "Auction Market," talks about the mechanism of the auction market that is attracting the attention of many and its present circumstances.

In the seventh chapter, "An Appropriate Attitude of Real Estate Appraisal Business," I have presented, based on my experience of running a real estate appraisal company for the last twenty years, some problems involved in the real estate business and what I think is its ideal picture in the entire business world.

My idea or thinking that you will read in this book may be biased. I hate gambling and therefore I cannot be too keen on the idea of making a lot of money on real estate or from buying and selling stocks. This might have influenced my impartiality.

But at least I can say that I feel very attached to real estate itself, and I have a hope that in the future real estate will be utilized in a more relaxed way. That is for sure.

What Decides Land Prices?

1

The Continued Slide in Land Prices

My Concerns About Optimistic Views

From around the summer of 2004 when I was writing this book, I often heard real estate business executives complain. "We cannot buy what we want because competition is getting too severe," they would say, or "The property that we wanted to get was 40 percent to 50 percent more than the posted price and we can hardly afford it."

In fact, newspapers wrote about average land prices in Japan's prefectures, as of July 1, 2004 (though the survey was released on September 21) saying, "The Pace of the Declines is Slowing," or even "Prices in Parts of Central Tokyo Begin to Rebound."

"The posted price of land" and "the average price of land" mean the land prices officially recognized and announced every year by the government. The government announces the prices of all spots throughout the country every year. I will explain it in detail in chapter 4.

Now, on September 22, there was an article in the newspaper *Asahi* that read as follows: "The average price of residential lots in central Tokyo (in eight inner city wards including Chiyoda and Chuo) has risen after seventeen years of decline. (Up 0.3 percent from the previous year). As for the national average, the pace of declines has slackened and the range of decline in price has be-

Table 1

Trend of posted prices before and after bubble period

(Year-on-year change)

	Central Tokyo (23 wards)		Entire Japan	
	Housing Lots	Commercial Lots	Housing Lots	Commercial Lots
1985	3.9%	12.4%	2.2%	3.8%
1986	10.0%	22.3%	2.2%	5.1%
1987	76.8%	76.2%	7.6%	13.4%
1988	44.1%	28.7%	25.0%	21.9%
1989	-5.2%	-0.9%	7.9%	10.3%
1990	0.4%	1.9%	17.0%	16.7%
1991	0.3%	0.6%	10.7%	12.9%
1992	-13.3%	-8.7%	-5.6%	-4.0%
1993	-22.2%	-22.5%	-8.7%	-11.4%
1994	-14.6%	-23.7%	-4.7%	-11.3%
1995	-6.8%	-20.0%	-1.6%	-10.0%
1996	-6.6%	-20.3%	-2.6%	-9.8%
1997	-4.4%	-14.8%	-1.6%	-7.8%
1998	-2.7%	-7.5%	-1.4%	-6.1%
1999	-4.8%	-8.5%	-3.8%	-8.1%
2000	-4.7%	-7.8%	-4.1%	-8.0%
2001	-3.4%	-6.1%	-4.2%	-7.5%
2002	-2.8%	-5.1%	-5.2%	-8.3%
2003	-1.9%	-3.4%	-5.8%	-8.0%
2004	-1.3%	-2.2%	-5.7%	-7.4%
2005	-0.3%	-0.5%	-4.6%	-5.6%
2006	2.2%	3.7%	-2.7%	-2.7%

come smaller for the first time in seven years for residential lots and in four years for commercial lots. The areas where prices rose for residential housing in central Tokyo used to be sporadic. Now, they are more common. The rate of declining prices in the Osaka and Nagoya areas is slowing, and it is being spotted in other major cities as well. Land prices might have reached the bottom."

Six months prior to that, the posted land prices of Japan released in March had shown similar phenomena (See Table 1). It was in 2004 that a ray of hope was seen in the real estate business.

Some people in the industry uttered a sigh of relief, in the perception that the brakes were being applied to the continual fall in land prices. At the same time, as mentioned before, there was a sign of intensifying competition for popular properties. The tide was certainly changing.

On the other hand, in areas other than Tokyo, Osaka and Nagoya, the range of decline in standard prices of land for both housing and commercial use was widening for seven consecutive years. When you look at the entire nation, there was no brake on the fall of land prices. The national average of standard land prices in 2004 marked a continuous decline for the thirteenth year.

The headline of the Yamagata edition of the same newspaper, *Asahi,* dated September 22 said, "Standard land prices continue to drop for seven years and this year by 4.6 percent, the largest ever." In 2004, some areas in Yamagata Prefecture, a rural area in northern Japan, dropped by 15.3 percent compared with the previous year and in adjacent Akita Prefecture, commercial lots at Nakadori in the city of Akita recorded a drop of 26.2 percent the largest in the country. At any rate, such views as "declining tendency of land prices has come to a halt" and "the movements of land prices are now twofold, urban and local," represented the predominant view among journalists.

But I could not help feeling concerned about those views of journalists. None of those newspaper articles discussed what exactly was happening in areas where land prices were rising or what was the reason for the rise.

In Tokyo, posted areas where land prices went up are mainly tony areas including Marunouchi, Roppongi, Shiodome, Shinagawa, Aoyama, Omote-sando, and Ginza. However, of those areas where prices went up, the reasons for the rise vary, and unless you clearly see them, you will not be able to tell how long the rising trend will continue and in what scope and as a result make a mistake in reading the price trend of the future.

Rising Prices Caused by Structural Changes or Demand Improvement

The reasons for the price rise in the urban area can be clearly divided into two. One is the rise in price brought about by improved urban infrastructure (Marunouchi, Roppongi, Shiodome, Shinagawa, etc.) and the other by improved balance of supply and demand (Aoyama, Omote-sando, Ginza, etc.).

Managers of businesses that import and market such quality consumer goods as apparel, handbags and shoes read that it will pay if they construct large boutiques on the main streets of Ginza, Omote-sando or Aoyama-dori. Not only Japanese managers but those of overseas had such conviction.

Overseas managers are well aware that comparing with the prices of Paris, London, New York and Hong Kong that have gone up over the last few years, prices of Ginza and Omote-sando had come down sufficiently enough to make operating in these prime areas profitable again. They considered while land prices in major foreign cities were on the rise, commercial land in central Tokyo has not gone up for a long time. Moreover, they seemed to have believed that the consuming power of their target customers in Japan will continue to rise.

In short, the price rise in areas as Ginza, Omote-sando and

Aoyama has come from the balance between an international comparison of land prices and an increase in consumer demand. We can also call it an upward pressure from business cycles.

In this regard, areas where land prices rose appeared in Osaka too, according to the standard land prices made public in September 2004. In the most colorful downtown area in Osaka, Shinsaibashi and its vicinity, what may be called "a foreign brands district" is being formed.

The popular downtown area of Shinsaibashi used to be Osakaites' favorite, Shinsaibashi-suji where roads are mostly narrow. But now, the foreign brands district is on a much wider street, Mido-suji a block away from Shinsaibashi-suji. This area is, similar to the areas in Tokyo like Ginza and Omote-sando, where the prices of land have gone up. In the long run, land prices at Shinsaibashi-suji, with the less attractive narrow streets, have been sluggish.

The rise in the prices of the land on the eastern side of Nagoya Station can also be considered a result of the change in the balance of supply and demand. Most directly, Toyota Motor, based in Nagoya, is constructing a big building there as planned. The Aichi world exposition in 2005, the opening of the new Chubu International Airport and thriving auto industry are also big contributing factors for the rise in land prices for the area. The changes in the supply and demand balance also raised the prices of land around the Fukuoka Station in Fukuoka Prefecture. But the factors contributing to the change are a little different from those for Tokyo and Nagoya.

Needless to say, the fact that a new bullet train line, the Kyushu Trunk Line which has been partially completed between Kagoshima and Yatsushiro, and which is expected to be extended to Fukuoka by 2010, does much to explain the price rises in this instance. But another factor driving prices higher is that Fukuoka and is vicinity have been active in recent years in promoting itself as a new window for the import and export of industrial products with Southeast Asian countries. The robust impact on warehousing and distribution is affecting the area's land prices.

Primarily, we can say land prices turned to a rising trend only when the balance between supply and demand has improved in the business cycle. In other words, we should not be happy to say that the prices of land have gone up unless it was a result of stronger demand for land than supply, rather than these rather unique circumstances.

Structural Change Brought About by Excessively Concentrated Investment

Let us examine the cases in which improvement of urban infrastructures caused the rise in land prices.

At Marunouchi in central Tokyo, prices were supported by the reconstruction of Marunouchi Building, the development of OAZO Shopping District, and turning Naka-dori Avenue that stretches from Yurakucho to Marunouchi into a street lined with famous boutiques. At Roppongi, land values were given a lift by the opening of two subway stations for two lines, a newly constructed skyscraper, Roppongi Hills, and redevelopment of the former Defense Ministry site. At Shiodome, the boost in property values came from another big redevelopment project involving the construction of such big buildings as Dentsu headquarters building and Shiodome City Center on the vast land used to be used by the National Railway. At Shinagawa, the rise came from a new Shinagawa Station for Tokaido Trunk Line and redevelopment of the station's eastern zone.

When a building that can attract a big crowd of people is constructed or a railroad station is renovated, retail stores surrounding it will also benefit by increasing their sales and investment return will be good. This, in turn, pushes up the land price as a matter of course. It is similar to a situation where you go to a noodle shop and order an expensive dish instead of a usual plain noodle to show off to a business colleague. Naturally, you will have to pay more. It is not because the shop raised the price but because your order was different from the usual one.

The same thing can be said of real estate prices. Your house used to be located at the third stop by bus from the railroad station. Now the subway line was extended and from its station to your home is now only a five-minute walk. As a result, the price of your lot that used to be ¥300,000 per *tsubo* (A Japanese unit of measuring land space that is still used commonly. 1 *tsubo* = 3.3 square meters) is now ¥500,000. The price did go up and it was because of the change in condition of the lot. This again is quite natural.

The rise in price of land as investment effect from big scale redevelopment projects is really remarkable. But we can also say that if such investment had not been made, there would have been no brake on the falling land prices. Or if additional infrastructural investment was not made, continued increase in land prices would not be possible in the future. The land price increase brought about by structural changes by such big investments could be limited in scope and transient. All this explains why I cannot be so optimistic about recent rise in land prices.

Declining Rent behind Redevelopment

Let us review the effects on prices of structural change made by big investments. Large scale investment in commercial buildings that was at its bottom in 1999 reached a peak in 2003. The total floor space of big office buildings (a building with more than 10,000 square meters of floor space) constructed in 23 wards of Tokyo in 1999 was 360,000 square meters, but in the year 2003, it increased to 2.16 million square meters. (See Table 2 by Mori Buildings)

Table 2

Supply of big buildings in central Tokyo (23 wards)

(1,000 sqm)

	Big Building Supply
1994	1,830
1995	920
1996	1,190
1997	740
1998	990
1999	360
2000	720
2001	910
2002	1,250
2003	2,160
2004	1,230
2005	1,030
2006	1,540
***2007**	1,190
***2008**	640

*Prediction - from Mori Building Report

That year, such top companies as Mitsui Real Estate (Shiodome City Center, etc.), Mori Buildings (Roppongi Hills) and Mitsubishi Real Estate (Marunouchi Building) actively invested and completed a number of luxurious buildings in many parts of Tokyo. In order to satisfy today's tenants, buildings must have the following elements: they must be new, they must be conveniently located near a railroad or subway station, they must be part of an expansive complex of buildings, and they must be big, high-rise buildings.

The aforementioned buildings in the Marunouchi, Roppongi,

Shiodome and Shinagawa areas of Tokyo meet those requirements and have attracted many tenants.

It was easy for the new buildings to convince tenants of older buildings to move to theirs. Buildings completed after Japan's economy slowed from the early 1990s, and land and service price fell, paid less for land, construction and lower interest as compared with those built during the 1980s, and therefore their rent could be set cheaper to attract tenants. Charging the same rent, the new buildings can secure profit whereas those built during the boom years of the 1980s inevitably suffer losses.

Nevertheless, tenants are actually paying higher rent for their super office buildings than they should be. They are willing to do so because commuting is easier, and buildings are spacious enough to integrate headquarters functions and subsidiaries into one place so that they can run their business more efficiently. It simply is new, functional and comfortable.

According to a research completed by Sanyu System Real Estate and Financial Institute in June 2003, the unit rent per *tsubo* (3.3m) for Building A at Shiodome was ¥37,000. The rent tenants used to pay before moving into Building was from 5,000 to 15,000 yen per *tsubo.* The rent for Building B at Roppongi is ¥28,000 to ¥32,000 per *tsubo* whereas that for their tenants' previous office space was ¥21,000 to ¥35,000. As against ¥45,000 per *tsubo* for Building C at Marunouchi, their tenants' previous rent was between ¥22,000 and ¥38,000. The rent for Building D in the same area is ¥50,000 per *tsubo* and their tenants used to pay ¥25,000 to ¥36,000 for their previous place. At Shinagawa, Building E's rent is ¥31,000 per *tsubo,* as against previous ¥15,000 to ¥25,000.

The result of the survey conducted on all the fourteen tenants at Building A mentioned above show that in spite of a higher rent, they are renting more space than they used to so that separated departments and subsidiaries could be integrated.

The construction rush of those new office buildings is having a serious influence on the real estate industry. For convenience sake, let us call the newly constructed building "a parent building" and the building that lost tenants "a child building." While the parent is thriving, it is causing a sharp decline of the child's rent and land prices surrounding the child building keep dropping. I think this phenomenon should be highlighted more.

Sanyu System Real Estate and Financial Institute carried on the research as to how the **child** buildings were doing after tenants moved to the **parent** buildings.

Of the fourteen **child** buildings from which tenants moved into the fourteen **parent** buildings mentioned above, only nine buildings managed to fill the vacancy two years later. The percentage of those buildings that failed to fill the vacancy was up to 35 percent. Some of them were even on sale.

The research was conducted not only on Building A but on tenants that moved into the other twenty-one **parent** buildings. Most of those **child** buildings were having a similar experience and the rate of unfilled space was 28 percent.

Also, generally speaking, there are often some phony elements in rent-out percentages and vacancy percentages.

For example, suppose we are in September and that Company A which has offices in Building X has a rental contract that expires in March of the following year. Now, Building Y aggressively sold itself to A by offering a free use of its space for six months until March and succeeded in convincing A to move to Building Y in October. As for X, it does receive rent for six months but the rooms are vacant. Accordingly, Building X keeps receiving rent and Y actually has Company A as its tenant. Theoretically both can claim that their rooms are being used. Tenants are doubly counted. Thus, the vacancy rate is actually lower than what has been disclosed. When many new buildings are constructed at a time and tenants actively move from older ones to the new, this is not uncommon.

Grandchild buildings that lost tenants to **child** buildings tended to refuse being surveyed and therefore comparison is not so simple. The non-occupancy percentage is recorded to be 11 percent which is rather low. However, as compared with the space used by tenants, the space used by the owner is twice as much and income from tenants' rent is not quite sufficient. According to the same survey, one **grandchild** building was on sale. Some of these **child** or **grandchild** buildings that used to rent out the whole building to one company is now leasing to two or three different companies at lower rent. They just have to lease their property out to smaller companies than their previous tenants.

Needless to say, there are a number of excellent firms among small businesses, but there tend to be a lot of problem enterprises as well. Smaller building owners, their backs to the wall, had no choice but to let smaller firms use their buildings. In areas where those buildings are located, there is a fear of worsening security. Such reality does exist behind completion of many attractive and modern buildings.

Forthcoming Crash of Condominiums

Many people throng to high rise buildings in Roppongi, Shiodme and Shinagawa every day not only for business but for spending rich moments of time at luxurious restaurants and leisure facilities. These people are attracted to the scene of the gorgeous world that could only be seen in such megalopolis like Tokyo. But even in these areas, there are people that are pressed hard by the decline of their real properties.

They are the condominium developers who have or are planning to build fashionable condominiums in the areas.

They have not been able to recover from the aftereffects of the go-go years of the 1980s, a period of low interest rates, high investment and strong economic growth commonly referred to in Japan as the "bubble economy." They are heavily indebted. In order to pay their debts back, they are eager to increase their sales. For that purpose they must continue constructing more condominiums even at the risk of unsold ones and secure immediate revenues. Should they cease to do so, they will face fund shortages in no time and there will be a danger of bankruptcy. It is a precarious existence.

Out of stupidity or desperation, they bought land in such areas as Roppongi, Shiodome and Shinagawa where prices of land were on the rise and built expensive high rise condominiums. In 2004 there were still many projects that had yet to be started. Thus, the pressure of all this increased supply remains big. With such pressures, a fierce dumping of high rise condominiums is underway.

A couple—husband in his 50s and wife 40s—who visited to see a model room of a certain condominium had a surprising experience. Attracted by a classified ad for a condominium priced at 80 million yen, they visited the site in the vicinity of Shiodome. But having a son who was to enter a university, the couple was thinking 80 million yen was a little beyond their reach. When they actually arrived at the site, it was a southern exposure, near the station, with a great view of the Tokyo Bay. Though very impressed by all these, they still uttered a sigh saying, "80 million yen!" Then the sales person whispered in a soft and kind tone, "Let's talk it over." When they went into another room, they could not believe when the sales person using a calculator said, "We would like to reward you for your enthusiasm. It's possible to reduce the price down to 60 million yen." To tell the truth, this story is fiction. But price cuts of 10 million or 20 million yen are nothing to be surprised at. Without such serious price cutting, the developer cannot compete in an environment in which all realtors sit on unsold properties. It is often said that once you buy a condominium, it will be a used property the following day and will be 30 percent less in price.

It is expected that dumping of these condominiums will spread and the prices of land in Tokyo will greatly be disturbed. Thinking of sales cost and possible risks, condominium realtors may try to sell buildings under construction all together. Then they might cancel buying vacant lots that they had planned to buy, and at the end they might go even further and sell the lots they possess.

This move will be seen in areas where high grade condominiums are built and they are also the areas for new urban office buildings and land where prices are going up. Oversupplies of condominiums can throw cold water on rising land prices in some parts of the areas. If land prices continue to fall, people will hesitate to buy property, and it will slow the return-to-the-city-center move. That, in turn, causes a vicious cycle of declining land prices.

If a real estate slump is to begin in the year 2005, it will be caused by a failure in high grade condominium business. In particular, it will start from central Tokyo that includes Roppongi, Shiodome and Shinagawa where new luxurious condos are concentrated. It will then spread to its adjacent areas and then to Osaka, Nagoya and Fukuoka.

Land Prices Will Become Half of What They are Now

As a result of construction rush of new buildings, uncompetitive smaller buildings will be pushed out of the market and disappear. This itself is a natural phenomenon in the capitalistic society. The problem is how fast the situation will develop. If it happens slowly, it may be acceptable. However, if older buildings are eliminated at a faster pace than conventional economic depreciation speed, its effects will be economically and socially too big to absorb. As I mentioned before, I cannot be too optimistic about a prediction that land prices will rise because of such factors as excessive concentration and a short-term phenomena of building construction.

It seems to me that Japanese have a deep-rooted fallacy about new buildings. They seem to think that if you expect land prices to soar, you should make use of an unused lot and put a building there. Seeing many buildings under construction with cranes on their rooftop, foreign visitors leave Japan with an impression that Japan's real estate business is thriving. But this is quite wrong. Building construction benefits construction firms, but with its completion a building supply increases. When buildings are in short supply, both construction and real estate companies will be benefited, but when they are in excess, it is construction companies that flourish and not realtors. They will have to face a stern reality that comes from an oversupply.

In 1987, public officials of the former Construction Ministry set up a private urban development mechanism to encourage both government and private sectors to purchase unused lots and construct buildings there. They reasoned that it is economically inefficient to leave unused land as it is. Some people criticized that it only created more positions for government officials, but I had to think that this was a wily strategy by bureaucrats. They are fully aware that land prices in Japan are still too high compared with the rest of the world. The more you build buildings, the cheaper the rent will become and that in turn lowers land prices. So, I imagine that they are taking advantage of people's misconception that the prices of land go up by constructing more buildings and pretend that they are working hard to raise land prices by increasing the number of buildings. Now that the site of the former national railways has mostly sold, a mass privatization of property over the past few years, cheaper land prices make it easier for the bureaucrats to reconstruct and redevelop the nation's land.

Whatever the bureaucratic agenda, the supply of commercial buildings continues to grow. The peak might have passed, but in the Metropolis large commercial buildings are still under construction and secondhand commercial buildings with much vacancy are also large in number. The secondhand buildings constructed during the bubble economy of the late 1980s can set their rent at a lower price so far as they can still pay back their loans. It is very possible that in the near future a tenant attraction battle might break out between used buildings and new buildings.

Such competition will then spread among new buildings at Marunouchi, Roppongi, Shiodome and Shinagawa, among powerful new building owner companies, then among buildings of the same owner and finally among used buildings. When the construction rush of new buildings is over, rent competition will intensify. Naturally, the value of those buildings themselves will fall, which leads to the reduction of land prices.

Thus, unless new demand is created among tenants, a structural change brought about by temporary investments will not stop the rent dumping race because tenants simply move from one building to the other.

Unfortunately, when we closely examine the areas where land prices went up, we find no places that enjoyed the rise in price as a result of improvement in the business cycle. Therefore, we can hardly expect that land prices will continue to go up for a long period of time and that the tendency will spread throughout Japan. After investment effects have weakened, prices of land will also weaken even in urban areas.

I think land prices will continue to fall for the next five years and if the pace of decline remains the same as at present, the prices could well be 50 percent of those in 2004. Needless to say, the story would be different if inflationary measures are implemented.

Under a scenario of inflation, even if you have no immediate plan of using the property, if you are prepared to pay yearly property tax, maintenance and repair expenses, it could be an effective investment to buy real estate expecting a future rise in its price.

Setting aside various expenses involved, real estate property does not rot even if it is kept for a long time. Besides, if you rent it out, you can offset property tax and other expenses and there will be no maintenance fee either. Here arises a false demand for real estate.

Should the government pursue inflationary policies, wealthy

people and firms with ample funds will actively invest in real estate. No matter how much genuine demand with actual use of the property lacks, as long as there is false demand, the rate of price increase could be higher than other commodities since there is no limit in false demand.

I speculate that foreign enterprises and big real estate funds that have been buying up properties in Japan in recent years have not been able to secure enough profits out of their investment in real properties. Yet, at the same time, they are afraid if they sell them they might not recover the principal investment. It is possible they will exert pressure on the Japanese government to pursue policies that ultimately may be inflationary. The Japanese government may think it is not a bad idea when they consider the amount of national debt they have issued.

The Influence of Fallen Land Prices

During the bubble economy, land prices of Japan were higher than those of any commercial sites in Asia other than Hong Kong. Industrial sites in China, Vietnam, etc. were far cheaper than those in Japan and the quality of their labor was comparatively good, that these countries attracted factories from Japan.

This move seems to be coming to an end. Production facilities that move overseas are now decreasing and financial institutions of Asia seem to be shifting their bases from Hong Kong and Singapore back to Tokyo. This shows that land prices of Japan have come down sufficiently enough to compete with other Asian countries.

I think, however, that it is about time for land prices to stop falling any further and to stabilize where they are. In order to realize it, it would be necessary to control supply and demand of real estate artificially.

But you cannot increase demand with policies. You cannot

ask a person who already owns a house to buy another house. Likewise, you cannot make a law to double one's tax if he does not use two *tsubos* where one *tsubo* of office space is enough for him.

On the other hand, it should be easy to reduce supply temporarily. All you have to do is stop accepting applications for new construction projects, at least for a period of time. But, this will likely result in hiring of very few employees for several years, and the impact could be felt in many other industries. What you can do is to present some conditions which will make it disadvantageous to construct buildings for a certain period of time and make it so that only those who think it will still be profitable can go ahead and construct buildings as they like.

Now, what kind of conditions can be presented?

1. Offer discounts on real estate taxes imposed on unused housing lots.
2. Have the state absorb the expenses needed to destroy unusable buildings, as it did with fallow rice fields.
3. Make it disadvantageous to construct new buildings by tightening the building volume ratio and building coverage ratio for a fixed period.
4. Delay the easing of restrictions on building volume and coverage ratios in designated areas.

Notwithstanding all this, what is important first is to establish among people that rent and land prices fall if supply exceeds demand by constructing too many buildings at a time. And now we must realize that we are about to be swallowed up into the whirl of falling land prices caused by oversupply.

In December of 2004, I gave a lecture at a periodical executive meeting of the Japan Association of Corporate Executives on the theme, "Land prices will fall by 50 percent in five years—problems involved as seen from the viewpoint of real estate appraisal."

I explained that rising land prices would not last very long, that they will turn to a falling trend when high-priced condominiums begin to depreciate. I further explained that it should not be surprising that in five years time land prices will be half the level now because of an excess in supply of real estate coupled with a slackened economy as a whole and declined demand for real estate.

I told them, "Even if your daughter asks you to buy a house for the birth of a grandchild, don't buy one! Instead, rent a nice house and pay the rent for her so she will be content."

I would like to say the same thing to the readers of this book.

The Perception of Land Prices vs. the Reality

To summarize the reasons behind the coming fall in land prices:

1. Further construction of large commercial buildings.
2. A price war of rental properties among owners of used buildings, which are dramatically increasing in supply.
3. Further increase of supply of high-rise, high-priced condominiums in downtown areas.
4. The growing supply of properties on the market that were once collateral for loans, now gone sour and repossessed by the financial industry.
5. A continued increase in the sale of factories and company housing.
6. Changing accounting rules for corporations causing further sale of company-owned properties.
7. A trend to convert commercial buildings into condominiums.

Table 3

Tokyo citizens' desire ratio for land price rise or fall (1997, 2003, 2004)

		Desire for price fall			Desire for price rise		
		Jun-97	Apr-03	Oct-04	Jun-97	Apr-04	Oct-04
Whole		84.0%	66.1%	58.6%	16.0%	33.9%	41.4%
Gender	Male	82.1%	64.4%	55.0%	17.9%	35.6%	45.0%
	Female	85.8%	67.8%	62.2%	14.2%	32.2%	37.8%
Ages	20s	90.6%	81.5%	61.5%	9.4%	18.5%	38.5%
	30s	86.7%	66.0%	61.0%	13.3%	34.0%	39.0%
	40s	80.1%	64.0%	55.5%	19.9%	36.0%	44.5%
	50s	79.2%	59.0%	56.0%	20.8%	41.0%	44.0%
	Above 60s	83.2%	60.0%	59.0%	16.8%	40.0%	41.0%
House owner or not	House owning family	77.0%	58.8%	50.8%	23.0%	41.1%	49.2%
	Non-house owning family	94.9%	88.9%	93.2%	5.1%	11.1%	6.8%
	House owning family in broad sense	79.7%	57.0%	50.6%	20.3%	43.0%	49.4%
Annual income	Below 5 million yen	91.9%	77.1%	67.7%	8.1%	22.9%	32.3%
	5 - 10 million	85.3%	60.6%	63.3%	14.7%	39.4%	36.7%
	10 - 15 million	80.5%	50.7%	46.5%	19.5%	49.3%	53.5%
	Above 15 million	58.1%	35.7%	29.7%	41.9%	64.3%	70.3%
Profession	Government	92.3%	42.4%	64.7%	7.7%	57.6%	35.3%
	Private (general)	85.9%	68.6%	59.5%	14.1%	31.4%	40.5%
	Private (finance, real estate)	55.6%	29.6%	36.4%	44.4%	70.4%	63.6%
	Self-employed	72.0%	44.9%	45.9%	28.0%	55.1%	54.1%
	Housewives	-	69.8%	60.8%	-	30.2%	39.2%
	Part-timers	90.9%	84.3%	75.0%	9.1%	15.7%	25.0%
	Students	86.4%	84.7%	83.3%	13.6%	15.3%	16.7%
	None	86.9%	66.9%	58.0%	13.1%	33.1%	42.0%

500 each male & female in Tokyo area, 100 each male and female of 20, 30, 40, 50, and 60 years old.

Table 4

Time series expectancy ratio of land-price fall

Tokyo

	Price-fall expectancy ratio
Jun. 1997	84.0%
Apr. 1998	84.4%
May 1999	75.6%
Apr. 2000	77.8%
May 2001	78.9%
May 2002	77.7%
Apr. 2003	66.1%
Oct. 2004	58.6%

Osaka

	Price-fall expectancy ratio
Feb. 2000	71.6%
Sep. 2002	64.5%

When I think of all these factors, I become more convinced that land prices will drop further. If prices continue to fall, Japan's economy and society will change to a great extent. We all know that financial institutions and other big enterprises were hard hit by falling land prices. We can even say the past decade of slow economic growth, what is commonly called "the lost decade," was caused by the decline in land prices.

But even with the situation as it is, people do not necessarily seem to expect their properties to appreciate.

How does the Japanese public feel about declining land prices? Sanyu System Real Estate and Financial Institute sent out questionnaires to 1,000 males and females to ask whether they expect price of land to rise or fall (a survey on people's perception of land price trends, conducted nine times in Tokyo and twice in Osaka. Table 3 shows the results of the surveys in Tokyo in 1997, 2003 and 2004).

Table 4 shows how the percentage of those who expect land prices to fall has changed since 1997. Taking a look at an overall picture, 59 percent of people still expect land prices to come down

Table 5

Top three reasons for disiring price fall and rise (Oct 2004)

Reason for wanting price fall	**Ratio**	Reason for wanting price rise	**Ratio**
To lower tax burden	19.1%	To raise asset value	33.6%
For easeir purchase of property	16.9%	Do not want value decline	17.9%
Cheaper the better	13.1%	To stimulate economy	15.9%

as of October 2004 even though more than ten years had passed since the bubble economy burst. In May 2002, however, 78 percent of people were hoping that the prices of land will drop, which indicates that people who expect the falling trend to stop and turn to a rise were increasing.

In June 1997 when we first conducted a survey of this kind, 84 percent of people were hoping the prices to come down, but between 1999 and 2002, the percentage of those who want the price fall went down to less than 80 percent, and in 2003 and 2004 the percentages were even lower.

Expectation for depreciation varies depending on attributes and locality. Osaka's expectation for price fall is smaller in percentage than that in Tokyo. Gender-wise more women expect land prices to fall than men. Men seem to be influenced by the conditions of their work place or their experiences and knowledge.

Taking a look at the age brackets, up until the year 2003, more than 80 percent of those in their twenties were hoping to see the price fall, but in 2004 little difference was seen between age groups. As for segments of those who own a house, rent a house or a broad sense of house owners such as those who can expect to own a house by inheritance, 90 percent of renters want land prices to decline. It is also interesting to know that more than half of house owners and a broad sense of house owners were expecting a fall in prices.

The biggest reason for them to expect the price fall is hopes for a decline in their tax burden, since a drop in the house value lowers tax rates and thus lowering the cost of maintaining the property. The inheritance tax is also a big part of the cost of owning a property. If you are thinking of buying more properties, you will expect real property acquisition taxes to be lowered along with the fall in property values. People do not hide that a lighter tax burden is the biggest reason for them to expect or hope for lower land prices. (See Table 5)

Now for the income brackets, 70 percent of those making less than 5 million yen a year were expecting land prices to go down, but the percentage gets smaller as their income increases. Among those whose annual income is above 15 million yen, now about 70 percent expect price increase. It is interesting to note that one year before, the percentage was 64 percent.

By occupation, 64 percent of private sector employees working in financial and real estate sectors desire price rises, while 50 percent of the private sector workers in the "general" category also expect land prices to go up.

As for young part-timers and students, approximately 80 percent of them were hoping the prices will fall and slightly less than 60 percent of elderely people with no jobs, as well as housewives, were hoping for price drops.

After all, despite the fact that the prices of land have fallen so greatly over such a long period of time, more than half the people still want the prices to go down. Both price rises and price declines have both merits and demerits, and I have not been able to decide which is better for the overall society, but I cannot agree with the view, expressed often by those I come into contact with, that falling land prices will lead the Japanese economy to catastrophe.

In the same questionnaire we asked for a prospect of land prices five years from now (as of Octobere 2004), and 36 percent answered "No change," 26 percent "Will be higher," 20 percent "Can't tell," and 18 percent "Will be lower." We also asked if they find it necessary to purchase land, to which 90 percent said, "No." This is an indicator to see a future trend of land prices.

2

Who Will Suffer Because of Lower Land Values?

What's Wrong with Land Prices Falling by Half in Five Years?

In the previous chapter I said the prices of land will drop by half in five years. I have been saying this for more than ten years, so many of my friends and acquaintances seem to remember my assertion very well. Recently, both posted land prices and transaction land values have stopped falling or even risen at some places and therefore, they seem to be curious about my posturing, whether I will change my views or not.

Young real estate analysts and real estate finance analysts are even harsher. When I see them at a seminar or other events, they often tease me by saying, "See, land prices have started going up." Without enough time to talk back to them, I manage to dodge the subject.

My contention that land prices will drop by half in five years has invited two kinds of protests.

One is that my bearishness is a self-fulfilling prophesy: "The prices of land fall because you say so." I just have to give a wry grin because I don't have such power of influence as the Governor of the Bank of Japan, who can send markets into turmoil with a simple utterance.

Another protest is: "If land prices go down further, what do you think will become of the Japanese economy?"

To that I have two answers. One is that even if the prices drop further, it shouldn't necessarily be bad for Japan's economy. The other answer is whether the economy of Japan might collapse or not, logically speaking land prices will have to go down. Just as one cannot call what is white or black, I cannot say it will not fall when it is bound to fall.

The people of mass media who used to come see me frequently to ask for my prediction of land prices don't seem to come these ten years. Perhaps they think of me as a dangerous person as I keep saying that land prices will fall.

When you say "Half the price in five years," the question is half of what. Half the price of a real estate property at its peak or half the bottom price after the bursting of the bubble makes a big difference in influencing the Japanese economy. When I think of the fact that in a little over ten years since the beginning of the Heisei Era (the reign of the current emperor of Japan), the value of commercial land in Tokyo which is the center of Japan depreciated to 20 percent of what it was at its peak, I get impressed at this country's economic power to endure such a situation.

During the bubble, companies and individuals, business corporations and banking institutions, the urban areas and the countryside, the rich and the poor, the young and the old, people all over Japan competed in real estate investment, mostly by borrowing money. If they hadn't borrowed money, their purchasing power would have been limited and problems wouldn't have expanded this much. As the saying went in those days, Japanese were truly "all realtors."

As a consequence, those who were affected by the fallen land prices, regardless of the amount, were really great in number. How deep the influence was can be seen from the fact that the prices of commercial land dropped to 20 percent and those of housing lots to 40 percent of their peak prices (all in Tokyo). In other words, a piece of commercial land bought for 10 billion yen at the bubble peak dropped to 2 billion and a housing lot that cost 100 million yen down to 40 million yen. The entire nation suffered the loss.

Then, how would it be five years from now?

As to the most of those who bought real estate properties at the peak of the bubble economy, the mess that they suffered after the price fall was just about cleaned up as can be seen from the fact that the outstanding balance of bad loans held by financial institutions has decreased. But for those who still hold properties, "half the price in five years" continues to apply. For example, the 2 billion yen commercial land is to come down to 1 billion yen. The loss incurred will be a billion yen. Considering that he invested 10 billion yen during the bubble, the loss in the future will be 10 percent. As for the housing lot for which 100 million yen was invested, its price has dropped to 40 million after the bubble. Then it will drop to 20 million yen. The future loss will be 20 percent of his total investment.

Meanwhile, those who bought commercial land in 2004 and 2005 are mainly domestic realtors, condominium traders, and the U.S. real estate and corporate reconstruction firms. Those who bought expensive, high-rise condominiums are a handful of successful businessmen mainly in the field of information technology and other new businesses. As compared with the huge population of professional and amateur realtors during the bubble economy, the number is minimal. These people are much more aware of their own responsibilities than many of those during the bubble, so they will not be affected so much by the loss from "half the price in five years." I am more concerned about banks that have blindly invested in real estate companies.

Have Financial Institutions Been Saved?

Japan's real gross domestic product (GDP) which was 442 trillion yen in 1989 (Economic and Social Research Institute, Cabinet Office) increased to 554 trillion yen in 2003. Considering that real estate prices dropped by 80 percent during a dozen years or so after 1989 when Japan's GDP was 442 trillion yen, the 10 percent expected from fallen land prices during a five-year period from 2004 and 2005 when GDP grew substantially should not be much of a problem. In addition, since those who are likely to be influenced by the drop in real estate prices are limited in number, "half the price in five years" may not be as serious as it sounds.

On the other hand, for financial institutions properties of whose borrowers have suffered as a result of fallen land prices, things are much more serious. They would hope to see a ray of light even in the slight tendency of price recovery in any parts of the country.

In an article in *Nikkei Shimbun* (Japan's leading economic newspaper) on August 16, 2004, we can catch a glimpse of such expectation by banks.

The article reported that the sales total of real estate collateral of 128 banks of Japan in the business year ended in March (fiscal 2003) exceeded the amount appraised by the banks by 18 percent. In other words, because of the recent rise in land prices, the real estate collateral held by the banks sold 18 percent higher than their initial estimate. They were trying to see evidence here that land prices had gone up to that extent.

Meanwhile, according to a study by Sanyu System Real Estate and Financial Institute, at the 2002 auction markets for the Tokyo District Court, where reposed collateral is sold, the ratio of minimum bidding requirements to actual sale prices (sale/minimum price) was already 137 percent (See Table 15, p. 132) This means that in 2002 real estate collateral was sold to bidders at 37 percent higher prices than the lowest sales price designated by the court.

Compared with the ratio at the Tokyo District Court, real estate collaterals for bad loans held by banks were sold at only 118 percent of the bank's initial estimates.

Why did this happen? Common sense tells us that it was not because land prices went up that the amount sold in real estate collateral was higher than expected, but because, as the Financial Services Agency points out, the amounts appraised by banks' own appraisers were simply too low.

After all, the rise in prices of certain urban areas alone has not been able to cover the downturn in value of all the banks' real estate collateral scattered throughout Japan. A temporary boom in limited areas is not enough to reduce bad loans that banking institutions still hold in large numbers.

The Merit of Putting Up Land As Security

When the price of land drops, banks that lend money for land get hurt. Receivables from borrowers will in no time turn to bad loans, thus putting pressure on business. Looking at the private sector alone, all such banking institutions as mega-banks, local banks, cooperative banks and credit associations suffered immensely and as a result, top-rated banks like Resona, Ashikaga, and UFJ found themselves bogged down.

With the inflated value of land during the bubble economy, financial institutions including mega-banks almost forced land owners to borrow money. So when the bubble burst and land prices kept falling for more than ten years, they had to go through a long period of hardship.

In chapter 3, I will explain in detail about the influence that the bubble economy and its collapse had on financial institutions. But now that fifteen years have passed since it burst, it will be interesting to see how banks have learned from their experience and how they have been changing their lending methods.

According to the Japanese practice of lending money on real estate, banks hold a lien on an entire company even when they lend money for a specific project. In many places abroad, the lender only has claims to the specific assets of the project, but in Japan, if the project does not produce the anticipated income and has a hard time generating enough to repay the loan, it is the entire company that is liable and must prepare a fund for repayment from its overall assets. As a result, banks tended to lend money with little true knowledge about real estate.

But banking institutions that followed such lending methods during the bubble economy now have a large number of bad loans. These days we often read comments by learned individuals and in the media articles saying, "Financial institutions were too dependent on real estate mortgages and disregarded the credibility of companies and their proprietors. Originally, money was to be lent only after ascertaining the borrower's credit worthiness, and not on the basis of collateral."

Katsuaki Tsuneyoshi, a former vice president of the now-defunct Nippon Credit Bank, offers a counterargument. One day when I was writing this book, I asked him a question about the failure of banking institutions. He said, "If your loan without collateral becomes a bad one and incurs a loss, you will be held criminally responsible for breach of trust and civilly responsible for compensating for the loss. A common practice in lending money is to give equal weight to both the company's credit worthiness and collateral." He also said, "Companies usually keep internal reserves in the form of various kinds of assets. When a bank asks for collateral on lending money, it is virtually demanding increased internal reserves. Companies that try to expand business without internal reserves cannot be trusted."

Meanwhile, Mr. Haruki Yoshida, the representative of Yoshida Economic and Industrial Laboratory and a member of the board of the former Industrial Bank of Japan, answered the same question with a slightly different nuance.

"When I was making decisions for loans some twenty years ago, it was common to ask for a mortgage on the proprietor's personal assets as a condition for a loan. But why is it necessary to secure personal property? I thought it unreasonable, because it could finish business managers completely, which is bad for the Japanese economy."

In the case of small businesses, there is no easy distinction between corporate and private assets. The question is how you think of collateral. It is a very delicate and fundamental question for Japan's economy. Those in the banking business may have many thoughts on how to interpret these remarks.

I myself believe that money should be lent upon assessing companies and their people. It is partly for this reason that I get apprehensive about the system popular today under which money is lent without examining borrowers: the same practice as in the bubble economy.

Concerns About Project Financing

The lending system that I am very concerned about is what is known as "project financing," including such schemes as "real estate non-recourse loans."

Project financing is, in simple terms, a loan system where money is lent based solely on the expected cash flow from a target project. Even if the project ends in failure, there is no need for the borrower to apply other assets for reimbursing. If the project defaults, you just turn in to the bank the failed property to offset the debt outstanding. There is no further obligation for reimbursement, no matter how big the remaining debt is or how much assets the borrower has.

What will the bank do with the property turned in by the failed borrower?

Needless to say, under the conventional lending system, if a project fails, one could lose all he has, and face difficulty in making a comeback. So it is understandable, for the purpose of invigorating the economy, that the system under which responsibilities are not pursued beyond the projects in question is welcomed in Japan in recent years. In the United States, project financing is common for real estate collateral loans. Some in Japan thought it was a good idea to simply import the system.

In the United States, however, banks have plenty of specialists who can look at real estate development or redevelopment projects and analyze their management plans. Only after thoroughly conducting due diligence, loans are issued.

Now the question is how much expertise Japanese financial institutions have to make accurate analyses of returns from real estate properties. Only recently some banks have become capable of doing professional analyses of real estate income. That is because they hired certified public accountants or outsourced whatever services they could not provide in-house. But most of them are foreign banks, and Japanese banks have yet to make their own systems fully functional. You could argue such a system was hastily brought in from overseas, without enough consideration for different cultures and customs.

Mr. Tsuneyoshi, whom I mentioned a little while ago, made the following remarks. When he did, he sounded regretful. "During the bubble era, financial institutions cut corners in analyzing the future prospects for real estate projects, even as they called the system project financing. Furthermore, they had an easy expectation that even if the project fails, they would be able to draw money from other investments they own and continue to make repayments. In other words, many of these cases were phony project financing in that they had relied partially on the credit of the entire company of the borrower. As a result, when things didn't go as they had expected, they ended up with mountains of bad loans."

Project financing is a lending system that looks exclusively at the future for the project, and not the credibility of the borrowing company or its management team. Therefore banks must carefully analyze the project. It doesn't matter what kind of good assets the borrowing company own outside of the project. They should not lend money based just on the name value of the borrowing company either. It means that you are lending money to a one-shot deal, without securing as collateral any assets other than the project itself. There are some people who say that such one-shot deals should be entrusted to real estate investment trust companies, which deal with real estate securitization business (explained later). They have much deeper knowledge of real estate than banks. It is not hard to understand that many experts and the mass media criticize the "collateral-ism" of financial institutions during the bubble period. But in the same token, shouldn't they also look at project financing, which has come under the spotlight lately? Under this system, banks decide whether to lend based on the possible outcome of the project, irrespective of the credibility of the borrowing firm or its management. We can say the collateral simply shifted from the land to a project in a short period of time.

To be sure, bankers during the bubble era made mistakes in reading the future price trend for real estate. The question now is how certain bankers are about the future prospects of projects when they consider financing the projects. Do they simply believe what people at investment trust firms, lawyers and CPAs have to say? And how much experience and what kind of knowledge do these professionals have?

I wonder why those experts and the mass media do not point out the danger inherent in project financing?

Isn't it true that what is important is to lend money based on "the quality of the people" or "the credibility of the management?"

Even in the field of financial business, good businesses come out of good human relationships, don't they?

I think whether you lend or borrow money, if things don't go well, you remember the faces of the people involved. Then you get encouraged and double your effort to overcome difficulty. Needless to say, the effect of pretty words is not universal. But if, at the very base, mutual trust does not exist, small mistakes can quickly develop into unrecoverable losses.

Since long time ago there has been a smart saying in the financial world: "The kindness to lend and the kindness not to lend." In today's ruthless systems such as project financing, if banks offer "the kindness to lend" and things go wrong, they suffer a big loss. And if they choose "the kindness not to lend," the borrowers only hold grudges against them.

There are a large number of vacant lots along thoroughfares in Tokyo that are the results of failed speculation moves by land riggers from the past. In the near future, many of these lots will be finally developed and most of them will try to raise funds by means of project financing. In many cases, financial institutions will form a syndicate to hedge risks in performing project financing. But syndication can easily be an excuse to evade responsibility. An old saying of the West states, "Everybody's business is nobody's business."

A Structure That Invites Evasion of Responsibility

Financing a "third-sector" project, those run jointly by private firms and the local government, can also result in the evasion of responsibility. These deals also will have to be financed by the project financing method.

Come to think of it, the Mutsu Ogawara development project, which involved creating a huge industrial complex at Rokkashomura in Aomori Prefecture in northern Japan was also financed by project financing. Now only a tiny number of private companies operate in the complex, surrounded by luxurious public facilities constructed during the bubble era. Instead of becoming a vibrant industrial area envisioned earlier, Rokkashomura has come to be known for its windmills, the nation's strategic oil reserve and nuclear fuel recycling.

A third-sector company called Mutsu-Ogawara Development was responsible for running the project but it went into bankruptcy in 2000 and left behind a debt of 240 billion yen. A new company called Shin Mutsu-Ogawara Co. has taken over its business, and even today, is trying desperately to attract private companies.

In this project, was there appropriate business analysis of the project financing scheme by Hokkaido-Tohoku Development Finance Public Corporation, the government-owned bank that was in charge of financing the project? The answer is clearly no. Its analysis was very poor. Furthermore, no one at the bank has claimed the responsibility for creating such an enormous amount of bad debts. Presidents of private financial institutions and other executives have been held liable for damages done to their banks, but for government financial organizations, no liability issues have been raised.

Japan Highway Public Corporation, Public Housing Corporation and Housing Loan Corporation are among these banks. If they continue what they have been doing, bad loans by public organizations will snowball.

Having dealt with many people from banking institutions, I have come to notice bankers tend to use project financing to keep lending money when there is a lot of money to go around. And when credit gets tight in the market and the banks gain advantage, they think they can change their loan agreements and start asking for corporate guarantees on the same loans.

But once you have a loan agreement, it is not that easy to alter it. Do you think companies would accept a request to write a promissory note a few months after a loan was made without such a note?

These problems are not confined among Japanese financial institutions. Project financing offered by foreign institutions doing business in Japan also appears shaky, because they don't have enough professional examiners who have a good knowledge of the Japanese real estate business.

I predict that within a few years there will be a large number of loan defaults as a result of project financing. When that happens, the lenders would have to cover the bad loans with the income from the failed projects. This would certainly put pressure on the lenders' cash flow.

J-REIT—a New Real Estate Financial Instrument

A great change has been seen in recent years in the field of real estate financing. What brought about this change is the spread of securitization of real estate, and particularly the introduction of real estate investment trusts. These funds are listed on stock exchanges, and are called J-REITs in Japan. Here I would like to explain this new type of real estate transaction in relation to land prices.

Whether private or commercial, people who are party to real estate transactions can be divided roughly into four groups: the owner, fund lender, user and the management company.

When we compare real estate with other commodities, we can cite many characteristics including: 1) the value of each item is much larger than those for other commodities, 2) if an item is owned by more than one owner, their interests do not easily match, often causing trouble at the time of buying or selling or renting the property. Therefore, in spite of the fact that they are an expensive commodity, and there are no legal restrictions, the historic tendency was for a single person to try to own a property or jointly with people whose interests are the same. Naturally, lenders of loans will try to avoid taking properties with complex ownership structures as collaterals. To cope with this situation, real estate investment trust was developed.

REIT is a method where a small amount of money is collected from each of the numerous individuals to create a huge fund, and with the money from the fund, they buy expensive real estate properties. Investors buy securities in a fund similar to shares in a company and draw income from the fund in accordance with the number of its shares.

It is a complex product, but if I have to explain what it is, I would compare it to investing in a studio, or one-room apartment. I think you have an experience of receiving a direct mail or a call from a real estate company, in which it says if you purchase an apartment for investment, the company will find a tenant for your property, and even if it doesn't, the company will guarantee the rent income for five years.

Let us look at how this works from the supply-side perspective.

The developer of the building with studio apartments buys a lot and builds an apartment building on it. It sells the building to a sales company and makes profit. If the sales company sells apartments to private investors, it also earns profit. In addition, it can manage the apartment and pocket fees.

Suppose an investor bought forty units in the building, each costing 20 million yen. The rent that comes into the investor's pocket will be, let's say 80,000 yen per month per unit. Now, the sales company receives, say 10,000 yen per unit as a "guarantee fee" for guaranteeing the monthly income for the investor. As for the investor, he or she receives, after paying the guarantee fee, 840,000 yen per unit a year (¥70,000 x 12 months), which is equivalent to 4.2 percent in annual interest (840,000 / 20,000,000) before tax.

Let's assume this was the calculation for each unit. If the

sales company fills thirty-five units out of forty, there will be no immediate gain or loss for its investment. This is because the total of 350,000 yen—the equivalent of five units' rent minus the guarantee fees—has to be shouldered by the sales company every month, but it receives 350,000 yen in guarantee fee (¥10,000 x 35 units) from the investor every month. In addition, the sales company receives maintenance charges either from the tenants or the owners (in case there are no tenants).

The sales company has to pay for the cost of finding tenants, of course, but compared with the risk of getting stuck with an unsold apartment worth 20 million yen, it can hardly be a big problem. All the company now has to do is to try hard to find as many tenants as possible beyond thirty-five units, so it can also make profit from managing the apartments as well.

It has become a lengthy explanation. Now, let's move on to J-REITs. For the seller of a J-REIT the owner of a commercial building can raise profit by selling it to an SPC (special purpose company, commonly known as paper company) and record the gain in his book. An SPC is also called a "vehicle," which is established for the purpose of securitizing real estate. In the example of the one-room apartment, this is the same process as the developer selling the building to the sales company.

A J-REIT guarantees dividends (rent) whether the properties in the fund are all sold or not. So, naturally, the fund asks for a fee equivalent to the guarantee fee in the one-room apartment example. So the J-REIT's ability to sell beyond the break-even point—selling at least thirty-five units in the previous example—is going to be scrutinized.

Furthermore, the J-REIT does not guarantee investors their original investments—the same as in the case of a one-room apartment. When land prices fall, those who invest in a J-REIT should not forget that their original investments (the appraised amount of properties in its portfolio) are not guaranteed even though their annual dividends (the rent income) are assured. The seller of the

J-REIT doesn't have to worry about what happens to the value of the properties in the fund. It should only be concerned about the annual income from the properties. Needless to say, if the property value goes up, it will even be better. But as I have said, I am skeptical the sellers of J-REITs care about it.

Even if a fund appears to be producing an attractive yield, the investment should be considered a failure if the original capital decreases in value.

It is quite natural in the market economy that once risk is passed on to individuals, the conduct of a company changes. In the case of the one-room apartment, the sales company doesn't care a bit if the selling price of the property goes down from 20 million yen to 10 million yen. The company has no risk of losing the principal of its investment. That means the company can make an investment in a new building without risking the original principal. So it will keep promoting the development of apartment buildings. Increasing the supply of buildings can lower the value of the initial investment if not done carefully. But since the company only has to worry about cash flow, and not about capital preservation, it has little incentive to act carefully.

J-REIT is a new product, the first one of which was listed on the Tokyo Stock Exchange in September 2001. As of the end of December 2004, fourteen J-REITs were listed on the stock exchanges in Tokyo and in Osaka, and their total market value amounted to 1.7 trillion yen.

Regarding the purpose and merit of real estate securitization or real estate investment trust, the 2004 Real Estate Securitization Handbook lists the following five points: 1) Diversification of fund procurement, 2) Giving liquidity to real estate, 3) Transfer of risk involved in real estate investing, 4) Improvement of financial standing, and 5) Fee business. I will attempt to explain each of these points in my own words.

1. First, the originator (the investor in the original real property) obtains an additional source of fund besides capital increase

and bank loans. Second, irrespective of the original owner's credibility, J-REITs enable him to raise funds advantageously in accordance with the quality of his property.

2. Instead of owning real estate, by holding securities even individuals with small amounts of money to spare can enjoy the same outcome as the owners of real properties. It also made reselling easier.

3. As for transferring risks involved in real estate, we need to look at two aspects. The original owner can raise profit at the time he sells his property to the vehicle set up for the purpose of securitizing real estate. Once he sells the property, he has basically nothing to do with the value of the property or the rent generated by it. Naturally, from the original owner's balance sheet, two items disappear—the property and borrowing. They were taken off the balance sheet.

For those who invest in real estate securitization products, REITs can be a good substitute when they wish to own real properties but find it difficult to do so for reasons ranging from insufficient funds to the trouble of property management. However, after purchasing the products, they must be aware of their responsibility which might arise from the change in the value of the original property or the fluctuations in rent. So, when prospective investors of real estate securitization products do not have enough knowledge of real estate, the distributors of such products need to explain to the buyers these characteristics of the products.

4. The original owner can quickly recover funds by selling his property to the investors in the vehicle to securitize real estate. This contributes to improving the original real estate owner's financial position. (This is related to paragraph 3.)

5. With the birth of real estate securitization products, new businesses, new firms and new products that are related to both real estate and real estate financing have come into existence. These include underwriters (firms that accept or underwrite stocks and securities; jobs for securities companies), credit-rating firms,

debt collection companies, real estate appraisers, and due-diligence business (asset assessment; see chapter 7).

6. If I may add some more, a new channel was created through which small investors can directly invest in real estates. Prior to this new channel, they could not deposit money in a bank, and ask the bank to use it to purchase real estate. Once the banks received the deposits, its distribution was the banks' job and the depositor could not ask the bank to do things like put half his deposit into real estate investment and the other half for buying government bonds.

So how did the new financial products, represented by real estate investment trust, bring a turning point in the world of real estate business in Japan? Here are the answers.

1. A new channel was created. Through this channel, funds can be raised for real estate development.
2. By breaking real estates into small portions, it was made possible for individual investors to invest in commercial properties.
3. By bringing together small investment funds into the vehicle of an investment corporation or a J-REIT, large-scale investments were made possible.
4. It is like a new type of real estate company was born, and this company is capable of meeting specific requirements of individual investors. By choosing a REIT that meets her taste, an individual investor can target a specific type of buildings that she is interested in, such as office buildings and shopping malls.

The advent of a new real estate financial channel that can gather small funds into a big fund to purchase properties has made it possible for the real estaste business to change.

J-REIT and Land Prices

Now, what influence do real estate investment trusts have on land prices?

With REITs, real estate companies no longer have to persuade bankers who are not well versed in real estate to raise money for real estate development. (This, however, is not applicable in a case in which a J-REIT, as an investment company, does conventional borrowing.) Real estate developers now can raise necessary funds by talking to real estate professionals. If the project is a profitable one, it should not take much time to collect funds. Nor will it be affected by the cash flow situations at banking institutions. You may think the emergence of J-REITs has a lot of merit for real estate companies because they can have multiple routes for raising funds now. But when you think of it carefully, you will realize that the traditional fund flow that went from small investor funds, banks, and real estate firms to real estate development was simply replaced with a new flow that goes from small investor funds to real estate investment trust to real estate development.

If that's the case, aren't funds from banks that are supported by bigger customer bases and are much more tolerant than real estate investment trusts a better and more stable source for real estate firms? It will be interesting to see how real estate investment trusts—with only a short history and little experience in tight money times—can collect ample funds from small investors at times of credit crunch.

Also, along with the economic climate of Japan as a whole, the performance of the entire real estate industry will also affect whether small investor funds will flow into the market. In the United States, REITs were utilized a lot when the liquidity of genuine real estates faltered in the 1990s, but toward the end of the '90s, the liquidity in the market rose and the real estate industry no longer had to rely on REITs so much. When the amount of total funds is shrinking, whether real estate investment trusts can maintain their superiority to other financial products for investment, thereby keeping necessary supply is difficult to predict. At any rate, it will be necessary to consider REITs as a product where the amounts of funds going in and out fluctuate greatly.

Secondly, there is a fear that during a period of ample funds, too many real estate investment trusts armed with lots of cash could invite excessive competition in the real estate business. As a result, a lot of unnecessary investments are made and bring down the earnings of the real estate industry. This would also hurt the performances of real estate investment trusts. With real estate investment trusts, the use of the fund gathered from investors is usually limited to real estate properties. This means a fund has to invest in properties regardless of the market situation. This could perceivably lead to a flow of excessive funds into the real estate market, similar to the one caused by banks during the bubble period. We have to make sure that bitter experience will not be repeated.

The history of real estate investment trust is still short and its total market base is not big enough. Therefore, we should consider it as an unstable fund compared with those from banks. Too much dependence on REITs can invite an undesirable rise or fall in land prices and rent. Which funds to use will have to be left to the judgment of individual enterprises. But the industry as a whole should avoid leaning on one source or another, and use them appropriately.

Although I have no intention of discussing here the adequacy of investing in real estate investment trusts for individual investors, I'd say they should be aware that it is a product that comes with great price fluctuations. It will be dangerous to make a judgment just by comparing its yield at the time of investment with that of the bank deposit. It may be wise to refrain from real estate investment trusts if you cannot face the idea that when you sell, the REITs value may be lower than at the time of the purchase. Even if the rate of return is good at the time of the purchase, if you lose the capital when you sell, you will not be a happy investor.

3

Banks and Appraisers during the Bubble Era

The Structure of the Bubble from Real Estate Appraisers' Views

Who really suffered the most when land prices fell? As I mentioned in chapter 2, they are the ones who bought expensive land by borrowing money. Along with those people, banks that lent huge amounts of money during the bubble economy are also still suffering. But it was real estate appraisers who played a part in creating the bubble, together with financial institutions. As the head of one of the real estate appraisal companies that are directly responsible for determining the land prices in Japan, I think it is worthwhile for me to testify what was happening in the real estate appraisal industry.

In September 1985, finance ministers and central bank governors from major industrialized nations gathered at Plaza Hotel in New York. The main topic was how the world can help reduce the twin deficits in budget and the current account in the United States, and the nations decided to jointly intervene in the foreign exchange markets. Under what's known as the Plaza Accord, Japan agreed to a policy to weaken the dollar against the yen, and expand domestic demand. After that, the Bank of Japan kept lowering the official discount rate until the beginning of 1987.

During this period, assets prices soared and a land price bubble formed.

Corporations and individuals rushed to acquire real estate. Even if there was no immediate use for land, people just bought it. The demand was fictitious.

Everybody thought they could realize huge profits in the future as long as they own real estate properties. If you have a new building and rent it out, you will have income from rent almost permanently. Real estate leasing became a very attractive business because you could raise rent every few years and earn profits without much effort. In addition, if you sell the property after some years, you could make a killing. For many, it became an investment business much more stable and profitable than their real jobs.

Corporations sought income by constructing commercial buildings on unused land they owned. After a while, it was not enough. They invested money to acquire vacant lots. If they used their own money, it might have been OK, but they kept borrowing to buy land. Banks did not hesitate to lend money. Public offices endorsed all of this. Thus, the entire nation fell into a trap.

Somebody Had to Tell the Banks

On November 10, 2004, while I was writing this book, a headline on a financial page of the *Nihon Keizai Shimbun,* the leading economic daily of Japan, caught my eyes. "UFJ Bank Obstructs Investigation. Asks Appraisal Firm to Inflate Asset Value in Client's Bad Loan Case."

When a bank evaluates a borrower's bad debt, it needs to have properties assessed high to make its own loss look smaller than what it actually is. But the value of most assets has dropped by half compared with the level during the bubble period. But it was banks and real estate appraisal companies that inflated the value of assets during the bubble era.

Let me explain from my own experience. It was around 1990, around the time of the transition from the Showa era to the Heisei era, and the bubble economy was at its peak. A housing loan credit guarantee company that was an affiliate of a major city bank was engaged in guaranteeing loans of its parent bank at 70 percent to 80 percent of the appraised value of the collaterals for the loans. But at the bank with which Sanyu System had some business, a considerable number of housing loan applications brought in from its branch offices were rejected by this credit guarantee firm. The reason was our real estate investigation reports. With strict appraisal results from my firm, the credit guarantee company could not guarantee the loans at applied amounts. Meanwhile, the same bank had its affiliated credit company guarantee similar loans. The loan applications rejected by the loan guarantee company were accepted by this credit company with no problem. For the same loan for a real estate property, one company could guarantee and the other could not. And the number of such cases was not small.

So the bank, without credit guarantee from the credit guarantee company, could not make loans fast enough and began to lose customers. One executive in charge of branch offices thought it was out of the question that a directly affiliated credit guarantee company was turning down the loans that the parent bank wanted to extend. He concluded that what caused it was Sanyu System's excessively strict appraisal of property prices. The executive called the president of the credit guarantee company and ordered him to stop dealing with Sanyu System, and use the real estate research firm that the affiliated credit company used. This firm, of course, appraised at high prices. What's more, the executive's order and the change in the top management at the credit guarantee company coincided.

I was astonished. If we could not do business with the credit guarantee company, our firm would be greatly affected. At the same time, if we appraised properties at higher value than what they really were worth to satisfy the parent bank, it was obvious that the credit guarantee company was going to be in trouble in the future

After thinking carefully, I decided the only thing I could do was to persuade the parent bank. The person I needed to see, I reasoned, was the president of the bank or the chairman of its board.

After studying the network of executives within the bank, I found out that the new president of the credit guarantee company was directly connected to the bank's chairman. So I went to see Chairman Hirose of Nihon Life Insurance where I used to work to ask for his letter of introduction. I recall he asked me if he should type the letter or simply write down some words of introduction on his business card.

I replied a business card would suffice, and with it in hand, I visited the chairman of the bank. I was invited into the reception room. I was greatly impressed when the chairman walked in by himself without being accompanied by even a secretary. I told him my concern about the latest development in the real estate market, including the problem of overpricing, the growing wealth gap between those who have real estate and those who don't, and what seemed to be irresponsible conduct of many banks. I touched a little bit on his bank's lending attitude, too.

For about an hour, he listened to me quietly. He even nodded to some of my comments in agreement. This is what he told me: "When I was the president of the company, our total housing loan balance exceeded that of the Government Housing Loan Corporation. Even now we are eagerly pitching housing loans. But I have been thinking we need to do something about the way we offer loans, so we will not be adding to the escalation of the bubble. But since now I am the chairman, I shouldn't stick my nose in management matters too much."

I was very relieved to hear what he said.

Later that day, despite his busy schedule ahead of a business trip to Hawaii, he kindly called, on my behalf, the presidents of both the credit guarantee company and the credit company. I don't know what exactly Mr. Hirose told the two presidents, but there is no doubt his calls helped.

The meeting was much more successful than I had hoped for. Initially, all I wanted to see as a result of my meeting with Mr. Hirose was a rumor about our private meeting would spread among the employees of his bank. I did not imagine he would go out of his way to personally call those executives.

A few days later, I met some people from the bank, including the executive director in charge of the credit check. Because of their busy schedule, the last thing they wanted to do probably was to meet someone like me, but that was part of my strategy. I tried to make the news of my meeting with the executive director—a very senior person—known throughout the bank. The strategy worked, and eventually, I was able to meet the executive whom I had really wanted to see. This senior banker told me to raise the appraisal figures of a few specific properties, but didn't cut our business altogether.

After meeting the executive of their parent bank, I went to see the new president of the credit guarantee company. We just exchanged niceties and didn't talk about any serious business matters. By then, he must have heard what I was up to from the folks at the parent bank. My position had also been well known among his subordinates.

Apparently, the new president held a grudge against me for some time for "intimidating him." After a few years at the credit guarantee firm, however, he moved on to another company, and we have been seeing each other on friendly terms ever since.

Later, the parent bank itself hit a rough time because of problems unrelated to real estate credit. But I understand the business of the credit guarantee company remains healthy even today. Of course, the conservative appraisal report from Sanyu wasn't the only reason for the company's success. The major reason was that the succeeding management team quickly and thoroughly disposed of their bad loans.

On the other hand, the business performance of the credit company worsened considerably. They closed the real estate loan department and the parent bank was brought in to extend financial assistance worth hundreds of billions of yen. When it didn't help, the parent bank sold the company to a foreign bank. I wonder how their employees thought about the management.

Appraisal Value As Desired by Banks

During the bubble economy, financial institutions were eager to lend as much as they could and fatten their loan portfolios. In those days, nobody ever thought that what they lent eventually had to be recovered. Or rather, recovering the loans was undesirable. That's because if the money was paid back, that would lower the bank's loan balance—something that needed to be avoided at all cost. This explains why borrowers, even deadbeats, never went bankrupt in those days.

So, the banks put on the market one after another loan products whose balances didn't decrease much in their early stages. Rather, products whose balances actually increase initially, such as fifty-year loans and two-generation loans, were introduced with much success. Occasionally, seriously defaulted loans were written off, but only in secret. In the area of never-ending growth, nobody was worried that bad loans would become a serious problem. They all believed minor problems would mend themselves.

It was about this time that the use of real estate appraisal firms became a general practice for appraising assets for collateral mortgage. That is because it became necessary for financial institutions to show to their clients and to the public they were not in conspiracy with real estate agents.

Prior to that, real estate financing was rarely offered and financial institutions were in advantageous positions. So they were able to request sufficient amounts of collateral that allowed them to recover their original costs in case the borrowers should become delinquent on their loans. So using appraisers to figure out how much the collaterals really were worth wasn't essential.

Now, let's look at what banks do to appraise the value of real estate submitted as collateral by their future borrowers. In fact, it varies from bank to bank but here are the common patterns.

1. To appraise within the bank.
2. To use a single real estate appraisal company.
3. To use more than one real estate appraisal company.

Appraising internally makes it possible for the bank to adjust the appraisal amount of the property to meet the need of the lender. It has both an advantage and a disadvantage.

The advantage is the bank's own appraisers can come up with amounts that match the size of the loans they want to extend. The disadvantage is the difficulty in securing good in-house appraisers. Their traditional practice of emphasizing employees who are born and bred within the companies made the banks reluctant to hire experienced appraisers from outside. But at the same time, it takes too much time to train appraisers internally. Furthermore, if too many loans are being extended at the same time, internal appraisers may have a hard time handling all of them. But when there is not enough work to do, they will just stay idle.

Interestingly, among banking institutions that had engaged in their own appraisal work, a big difference in results is seen depending on whether the appraisal department was part of the sales department or the auditing department. It's easy to understand why.

When a bank hires an outside appraisal company, who has more influence in hiring often determines the result. If the sales department is in charge, the bank tends to pick a company known for easy assessment. If the examination department has more say, the bank could choose a company known for strict assessment.

Needless to say, banks that had lax appraisers ended up with more bad loans.

The reason for using more than one appraisal firm was partly that some firms may not be well informed about particular areas, or have strengths or weaknesses depending on actual properties they have handled in the past. But some banks also have more than one firm report results to them so they can choose what they like among a few different numbers.

In the past, banks obviously thought they could change appraised values of properties in order to best accommodate their lending activities.

It may be hard to believe, but some banks, together with reference materials for the property, used to send to appraisal companies a document with "a requested appraisal amount for the property." In practice, it was an instruction for the appraisal amount, rather than a request.

The following is the example of such an "instruction" that we actually received.

"The bank can presume that value of the property that we have asked you to appraise is approximately 100 million yen. Watching the recent land price trend, the value will almost double in a few years. Suppose the loan-to-value ratio (normally less than 70 percent) is set at 100 percent, we are confident that we would recover the full amount on a loan of 100 million yen. Now, the person who applied for the loan is very fond of playing golf. We would like to lend to him 20 million yen on the same collateral so that he can purchase a golf club membership. In addition, since he has constantly been successful in stock transactions, we would like to extend a 30 million yen loan to him as his stock investment fund, also on the same collateral.

So, the total amount of the loan will be ¥100,000,000 + ¥20,000,000 + ¥30,000,000 = ¥150,000,000. Under our regulation, the loan-to-value ratio for real estate collateral cannot exceed

70 percent, so calculating back, we would like the property to be appraised at 220 million yen."

Imagine our surprise. No matter how hard we tried, we could never come up with that kind of figure. So, of course, we turned down the business. When we notified our decision to decline, the bank's employee in charge said in a disgruntled manner, "You are not the only appraisal company. There are a number of better firms." To them, a good appraisal firm is one that comes up with whatever figures they desire to see.

There were appraisers who gladly complied with those incredible requests. Since there was a method by which the appraisal fee was calculated as a fixed rate of the property value, the higher the appraisal, the larger the fee they received. Some appraisers were deprived of their licenses when they went too far in gouging fees.

Around that time, I insisted that if banks were so anxious to increase their loan amounts, they should internally raise the loan-to-value ratio for individual loans from the customary 70 percent to 150 percent or whatever they desired, based on the customers' credit worthiness. I thought that it was not the right way to use the appraisers to change the appraisal values.

If the banks don't know the true value of a property at the time of lending, how, in the future, can they compare the amount of the loan and the going price of the collateral at the time when the loan was extended?

Things often don't work out as you think they should. Because we refused to be "flexible" in our appraisal work, the revenues of Sanyu System went down during the bubble economy.

Cleaning Up the Result of Appraisal Padding

Now, let us consider what effects inflated appraisal brought about.

If we submit an appraisal report that gives a property only worth 100 million yen an inflated appraisal value of 220 million yen, 1) the bank will naturally have both the buyer and the seller sign a 220 million yen sales contract, 2) and will lend the buyer 150 million yen which is 70 percent of the contract amount. 3) The sales price of 220 million yen will be reported to the Real Estate Appraisal Association as a case example. The price will then be formalized for that location. 4) Now, another appraiser was asked to appraise a property located near the property that had been given an inflated value. How would he make an assessment? If a nearby lot is priced at 220 million yen, he would certainly use that price as a reference for appraisal of his client's lot. The owner of the lot next to the inflated property then will naturally try to sell his lot not for 100 million yen, but for 220 million yen.

Thus, real estate prices were not decided by supply and demand but rather by the amounts of money banks wanted to lend. This is how the bubble kept growing. I don't think any economic theory can explain this.

During the bubble period, financial institutions not only asked for padded real estate appraisal, but kept pushing appraisers to do the work quickly because they needed to beat other banks in closing their loans. Needless to say, trying to do appraisal work too fast can cause mistakes. We often declined appraisal requests that didn't allow us to spend enough time to do what we believed we needed to do.

The banks that we declined must have gone to other appraisers, of course. Of course those appraisers only did sub-par work, and the results were not good. Even now, we don't usually accept jobs that come with short deadlines. That's because I immediately grow suspicious of the intent of the financial institution.

Having witnessed such behind-the-scenes practices of banks, I had grown concerned about their future. From around 1983, I talked to a number of bank executives and employees about such conduct and expressed my concern. I also talked to the members of the press. I went as far as to say financial institutions should not engage in real estate loan business. But the people who heard me were simply appalled. Someone even said to me, "If I said something like that in my office and put it into practice, I will be branded as an incapable sales person and will be finished."

Since that time, I have been repeating the same belief as if that was the only thing I cared about: In five years, Japan's land price will be half of what it is now. Actually, in the past twenty years or so, we experienced two or three periods during which the land price halved. When it didn't fall by half, it fell by 30 percent or so. In other words, I continue to make right predictions, based on my everyday work experience. Because of my work, I have always been watching carefully to see when the turnaround point for land prices will arrive. I would love to declare such a shift and explain the reasons for it faster than other experts. But I don't see any signs of such a turnaround. Rather, I dare say that five years from now, the fall of 2004 as I write this book, the land will very likely be half of what it is today.

Two Appraisal Prices

In 2004, experts began to say that the banks had turned the corner in writing off bad loans. Around this time, appraisal firms found themselves facing the problem of "two appraisal prices."

For appraisal requests from banks, if they have anything to do with bad debt, completely different results are expected, depending on which department of the bank the request comes from. Even within the same due diligence department, the group that is in charge of dealing with the Financial Services Agency wants the appraisal result to be as high as possible so it can help make the bank's bad loan amount look smaller. The group in charge of bad debt collection, meanwhile, wants a low appraisal value so it can unload the property as quickly as possible. The group could also claim credit if it can sell the property with a low appraisal value at a higher price. If you own a property worth 100 million yen and had it appraised for 80 million yen, you could sell it for 90 million yen and still be praised for your effort. It doesn't matter you sold it for less than the market value. The appraisal company will have to be careful not to be pulled into schemes like this.

Occasionally, appraisal reports with such inflated assessments—whether they were made intentionally or by mistake—come to light during an annual inspection by financial regulators, or when a third party is brought in to conduct due diligence after the original debtor goes insolvent. Even when it was discovered as a result of an annual inspcction, the bank sometimes has discretion in deciding whether to make it public.

Needless to say, if individual employees of the banks and the appraisers are in conspiracy, inflated assessments will usually go unnoticed. The failure of the debtor may bring such cases to the open, but by the time a bank begins to see several cases of insolvency among its clients, the bank itself must be close to its own failure. It will be too late for the bank to file a complaint against the real estate appraiser or to its own employee.

When an appraised amount is inflated, it is usually the bank that eventually gets into trouble. The issue is it usually takes a few years until such a problem surfaces. Therefore, banks must be very careful in choosing the right real estate appraisal company.

Earlier, I talked about a bank-affiliated credit company that got into trouble and was eventually sold to a foreign bank. This company used an appraisal company that employed four or five former employees of the parent bank. It is not hard to imagine appraisal work done by this company was far from accurate.

Behind the bad loan problems that have devastated many financial institutions for over a decade, there were often collaborations between bank employees and irresponsible appraisal firms, or hiring of incompetent appraisers by the banks. These problems, unfortunately, could not be uncovered until much later.

I tend to think picking a real estate appraiser is similar to picking a home delivery service.

In deciding which delivery company to hire, you will consider various aspects of its service, including whether it will send someone to pick up your package, if the company has an office nearby, how much the charge is going to be, and how soon the delivery will be made. But you don't usually think about what kind of service the company provides to the receiver of the package.

One day when I got home at around two in the afternoon, I found two notes in my mailbox. One was from the post office and the other from a major private delivery service. Both notes essentially said the same thing: since I was out, they took the packages back and that I needed to call to arrange for the time of the second delivery. But when I called them to say that I would be home for the rest of the day but be out the following day, their responses were different. The private company said it would deliver the package immediately, but the post office said I had to wait until the following day. When I said I would be out the following day, I was told it was my problem.

This sort of thing happens in part because most senders assume all delivery services are the same and do not think of the receivers' convenience.

When financial institutions select an appraiser, they may consider the cost and speed of the appraisal service but not what will be in the report. In other words, they don't pay much attention to the quality of the work.

If it is about a package delivery, the receiver can simply ask the sender to use another courier the next time. But with real estate appraisal, banks don't even notice a problem exists until the debtor goes bankrupt. If the appraiser itself fails, even that cannot be done. I would like to emphasize that if you are choosing a real estate appraiser, you should not make decisions based simply on the terms and conditions of the contract.

Luckily, my company or I did not buy any real estate property during the bubble economy. I think banks stayed away from me because I was often quoted in the media as saying that land prices would fall because of the absurd conduct of the banks. If they had come to me with offers for attractive properties, I might have fallen for them and invested my own money, forgetting my public position. I now thank banking institutions for bypassing my door. I was really fortunate.

Aftermath of Lending Competition

One may wonder why financial institutions, with so many ultra-elites among their staff, could do such foolish things.

Banks are often ranked according to the amounts of their total deposits. But no matter how big their deposit portfolios are, they cannot earn profits unless they make good use of the money by lending or investing smartly. When the economy and markets are healthy, banks have many customers who want to borrow money. So whatever they gained in deposits could be recycled immediately and pushed up the banks' loan balances and profits.

After World War II, banking institutions in Japan always had enough customer demand for their funds and did not have to compete with other banks so much. They could stick with their business plans and they did just fine. Even when some of them tried hard to beat rivals in getting new customer accounts, the results weren't too impressive. So, their positions in the financial industry league table stayed fairly stable, unless something totally unexpected happened. Under the so-called convoy system, where the government coordinated the operations of the industry to make sure everyone grew together, it was more important to cultivate ties with bureaucrats and carry favor with them.

However, after the Plaza Accord in 1985 mentioned earlier, financial institutions started competing furiously with each other as Japan entered an extraordinary period of monetary easing. For most bank executives and employees, the experience resembled nothing they learned in economics textbooks. Simply lending money didn't work anymore. They had to lend a larger amount of money to a better customer at a higher rate. In order to accomplish this, they were constantly under pressure to make decisions more quickly than other banks and inform their clients as soon as they were made.

But among their existing clients, there were only so many customers who were willing to borrow on the terms and conditions that the banks now desired. Unless the banks could find new borrowers, they could not increase the amounts of lending that would bring in additional profits.

So they looked around hard and found a new business: real estate.

Real estate prices in Japan had risen constantly except for a short period immediately after World War II. Even if prices went down temporarily, they recovered fairly quickly, in three years or so. This meant banks could use real estate as collateral for long-term loans with durations of five years or more with little risk. Besides, when there weren't enough real estate properties in the market, you couldn't increase the supply by importing, like you did with iron and oil. That meant that a price rise was inevitable. Lending on land as collateral was completely safe, the bankers reasoned. And as if it wasn't enough, real estate loans could be offered to both individuals and companies. "OK, this is it" was the conclusion of so many bankers.

For banks, the merit of lending money on real estate as collateral was as follows:

1. It had a good collateral value.
2. The amount of each loan was generally bigger than those using other assets as collateral.
3. A big amount of loans keeps the bank's cost low.
4. Higher interest can be collected compared with loans

using other collateral objects. (When I come to think of it now, it is strange that higher interest was charged on real estate loans if people really believed real estate was a safe collateral.)

5. Real estate is safe because the debtor cannot hide it without the knowledge of the creditor, and he/she cannot run away with it.
6. By placing a mortgage on real estate property, receivables can be secured.
7. Real estate does not rot or depreciate in a few years.

Because of these reasons, financial institutions rushed to offer real estate loans.

Lending money on real estate only (Land and buildings) as collateral started around 1930, at the time of what was known as "Showa Depression." The first bank to enter the business was Nippon Kangyo Bank, which offered loans on farmland as collateral. It was during the 1930s when housing loans similar to what we have today were first offered by private banks. Before that, banks might have lent money on the land borrowers already owned, but nobody could think of making a loan on a property that the borrower was yet to own. It was common sense during those days that only rich people could take out loans.

So real estate collateral loan is a financial product with a relatively short history. And this product transformed grotesquely during the bubble economy in the late 1980s and the early 1990s. Banking institutions did not simply offer loans at the request of borrowers. They started by persuading real estate owners to sell their properties, and as soon as they agreed to do so, the banks started looking for the buyers so that they were there to lend money for the purchase. In this way, the banks could increase the total amounts of their interest-bearing loans, while at the same time, get the seller to deposit the proceeds from the sale of the property that would boost their deposit balances. Furthermore, brokerage fees roll into the realtors affiliated with the banks. These banks were all part of broader corporate groups, which had various functions including real estate brokerage. In reality, banks were playing the role of the realtors.

This, however, later developed into a situation where borrowers who could not pay back their debts complained that their banks forced them to buy properties that they hadn't really needed. Some banks were held accountable for their dubious conduct.

The financial health of banks today varies greatly, depending on their attitude toward real estate loans during the boom era. There were a few banks that completely steered clear of lending on real estate. During the bubble era, these banks that were cautious about real estate collateral loans were called out-of-date, inflexible, or outright stupid. Their efforts have been redeemed. Today, they are praised as being sound, safe and principled. People's opinions do change dramatically.

Loan-to-Value Ratio: 120 Percent

Even during the bubble era, the banking industry had a rule that required banks to limit the amount of each loan to 70 percent of the value of the collateral. Whether banks actually followed this rule affected their performance today considerably. The idea of loan-to-value ratios had been in existence since the beginning of time, from the ancient days. They were considered rough measure for safely recovering investments in case the borrowers fell behind in their debt payments. According to the internal rules of a certain major bank in the prewar days, the loan-to-value ratio was set at 90 percent for government bonds, 80 percent for municipal and corporate bonds and 70 percent for shares of publicly traded companies. If the duration of the loan was three years or less, the bank was able to recover the cost of the loan regardless of small fluctuations in the value of the collaterals.

After World War II, most banks customarily used the loan-to-value ratio of 70 percent on loans using real estate as collateral. However, during the bubble period, real estate prices surged by 50 percent to 100 percent just in a few years. (In fact, during the single year of 1987, the prices of land for both commercial and residential use in Tokyo went up by 70 percent according to key government statistics.)

In view of rising land prices and intensifying competition among financial institutions, some banks eased their loan-to-value ratio and started using 100 percent or even 120 percent. For reasons unknown to outside observers, loans worth 20 percent more than the value of their collaterals were commonly offered by banks. Such a practice seems simply absurd today, but few people questioned it in those days.

As I mentioned before, even those banks that claimed to use the 70 percent ratio often asked their appraisers to pad the value of the properties so that they could lend the amount that they desired. The appraisers who went with these banks and manipulated real estate prices should also be held responsible.

Furthermore, banks often rushed to close loans after accepting applications from customers. In order to reduce the time and cost of examining loan applications, banks sometimes followed the advice of foreign consulting companies, and under the banner of "quick response," put the due diligence department under the sales department.

Banks have excellent planning departments of their own, so it is not clear why they entrusted such a life-threatening matter in the hands of unfamiliar consultants who were not versed in the circumstances of this country.

From what I understand, when a top executive of a bank is appointed, he often asks an outside firm to come up with new ideas so that he can show them off as if they were his own. Maybe shuffling around the due diligence department was among such ideas.

The Lesson from the Bubble Era

As of this writing in 2004, it has been fourteen years since the collapse of the bubble economy that resulted in heavy declines in stock prices. But the lesson from the frothy market era is still very much meaningful for today's economy. Banks today sit on huge piles of surplus cash as they can't find enough borrowers. Many banks and life insurance companies have too much money on hand that they keep channeling the funds to Japanese government bonds, even though they are well aware of the risk of investing so much in a single financial vehicle. The land bubble of the past has simply returned in the form of a government bond bubble.

Now, I would like to examine how banks in Japan have treated their due diligence departments since the beginning of the bubble era. I would also like to look at what influence they have had in the creation of the bubble, and on snowballing of bad loans and the subsequent collapse of the boom economy.

After the bubble economy, we often read in newspapers such headlines as "Bank A Revives Diligence Department" and "Bank B Upgrades Due Diligence Section," These headlines remind us just how much the banks were pushed around by consulting firms, whom I believe had a big role in escalating the property bubble.

The competition to boost loan balances was not limited to banks, but it involved non-bank financial institutions. Non-banks cannot accept deposits from the public, but they can borrow money from banks and lend it to individuals and corporations at higher interest rates. Leasing firms, real estate finance companies and consumer finance companies were among the particularly eager players. Needless to say, their attitude in lending was different from that of banks. They were more flexible in their lending policy, and they could do almost anything, as long as the loans brought in profits. The way they offered loans was such that they loosened the loan-to-value ratio beyond the 70 percent benchmark, promoted long-term loans with durations that span from fifty years to 100 years to nearly eternity. As long as interests were paid every month, these financial institutions didn't push for the repayment of the principal.

Unless they developed products that could compete with such aggressive loan products, banks would eventually give in and lose valued customers. So, most banks relaxed the terms of their lending as much as possible. At the same time, banks were willing to offer financing to those non-bank institutions. The outcome of lending was usually miserable. Many of Japan's second-tier banks, including long-term credit banks, city banks, regional banks, and credit unions also resorted to similar lending practices. Cooperative banks and credit associations were no exception to this tendency.

Are Foreigners Repeating the Bubble?

During the bubble, financial institutions tried to approve loans as soon as possible and as much as possible so that they wouldn't be a loser in the competition with rival banks. As a result, when they asked real estate appraisal firms to evaluate collateral properties, they asked (or directed?) for far higher amounts than the market value of the properties, and asked to finish the reports as soon as possible.

A thorough examination of auction documents reveals that many secondhand condominiums worth just 40 million to 50 million yen were mortgaged for more than 200 million yen. When you face such reality, you will be convinced how abnormal the situation was. (Detailed analysis of the auction market will be made in chapter 6.)

I would like to repeat once again that what looks abnormal to people today was nothing strange to the people in those days. But the consequence of such conduct is now very obvious. The number of nationwide banks tumbled just a few from over ten a decade or so ago.

In Japan, however, there still are companies that are behaving very similarly to what many banks did during the bubble era. They are foreign banks and real estate firms.

Generally speaking, a large part of the compensation for professional staff at foreign companies is based on their performance. And their performance is often measured by the amounts of loans extended to clients, overall loan balances, and prices of the real properties purchased. Amid the poor demand for funds from customers since the end of the boom period, banks are desperate to obtain new customers. Naturally, foreign banks are also caught up in this competition and their Japanese staff work hard to meet their performance targets. These people are under intense pressure: if they don't work hard enough, they may face pay cuts, or worse, job losses.

After all, they too, like their Japanese counterparts during the bubble, have come to wonder if they can have their appraisers inflate the value of the properties to be used as collateral so they can boost their loan amounts. They insist that if the appraised amount is the same as the going price, they cannot lend what the borrower wants. Or if their companies themselves are buying the properties, they insist, unless they can offer better than the going prices, they will lose out in the auction and lose the opportunity to buy the property. In fact, we at Sanyu received a request from a foreign firm to pad our appraisal

What seems very common among foreign companies is that the evaluation of their staff's performance is made in the early stages of projects, rather than on their final outcome.

Suppose a loan valued at 70 percent of the value of its collateral is successfully closed on a property appraised at 10 billion yen, thanks to the effort of a Japanese employee of a foreign company. But actually, the real value of the property was 8 billion yen. The amount had been intentionally inflated to 10 billion in its appraisal report. Meanwhile, his boss in New York or London has no way of knowing the property's real value was 8 billion.

The employee's immediate boss in Japan is very happy because his employee was successful in beating their competitor, and was able to lend 7 billion yen, instead of 5.6 billion—the appropriate loan amount if the property was fairly appraised. If they could repeat such aggressive lending practice, the performance of the Tokyo office of the bank will keep rising sharply. The Japanese employee gets a special bonus and a promotion and his boss is offered a better position at the home office.

Now, five years later, the borrower of this loan gets into trouble. In order to recover the loan, the foreign bank tries to repossess the collateralized property and sell it on the market. The land price has remained flat for the last five years. The bank realizes it can only receive 8 billion yen for the property, rather than the 10 billion they have counted on getting. This foreign bank had thought that they would earn good profits by collecting a reasonable amount of interest on its loan for five. Instead, at the exit, they realize they have suffered a big loss. Whose fault was it?

It was the Japanese employee who had set up the loan. But this man is no longer with the company because he produced good results over the years and has been recruited by another foreign company that offered him a better pay. His Japanese successor is now under pressure to sue the appraiser for doing a sloppy job just to show the home office that he is doing his job. But the appraiser is not capable of reimbursing such a big amount to the foreign bank. Besides, the prospect is dim for the bank to win the case because it was its own former employee who had instructed the appraiser to report that amount.

As such, foreign companies are now repeating exactly what Japanese financial institutions did during the bubble era. The difference is at foreign companies, it is hard to hold people responsible for their conduct because they jump from one company to another rapidly in search of better compensation and benefits.

A scandal at the Japanese unit of Citibank in the fall of 2004 is a typical case.

A branch office of the bank in central Tokyo was accused of selling highly risky products to elderly investors who were in their seventies or above. According to the investigation by the Financial Services Agency, the bank had also allegedly opened a savings account for a member of a crime syndicate, ignoring its obligation to report such cases to the police. The bank offered loans to small businesses in return for underwriting privately placed bonds. Such arrangements are prohibited by law. The bank was also allegedly engaged in selling real estate and art objects for fees, something a bank branch is prohibited from doing.

Meanwhile, the head of the Japanese operation of the bank left Japan to take up the position as a director of Columbia University. The bank's general sales manager in charge of private banking also moved on to another foreign bank. Citibank survived the case relatively unscathed, with the suspension of the private banking business at just four branch offices for a year, and the subsequent loss of its private banking license. If something similar had happened at a Japanese bank, it probably would have been forced out of business.

At any rate, the central issue as foreign companies involved in real estate lending is that the evaluation of employees' performance is based on the amount of loan origination, rather than the eventual profitability of their projects. Since the turnovers of employees at these companies are so high, they cannot wait to see the outcome of projects to evaluate the performance of their employees. It is one negative aspect of the employment system where, unlike at Japanese companies, life-long employment is not common.

In recent years, my company is experiencing a situation very similar to what we went through during the bubble. In the late 1980s and early 1990s, requests for real estate appraisal from Japanese banking institutions all but vanished because of my honest view of the market. Similarly now, our business with foreign banking institutions is on a decline. But we are not worried. Two or three years from now, when bad loans held by foreign companies come to the surface, I believe my company's business will pick up again, just as it did after the burst of the bubble.

I would like to emphasize here that some foreign banks have indeed engaged in dubious lending practices in recent years, but the scale of such business is tiny compared with the highly speculative lending activities that many Japanese banks conducted during the bubble economy. Needless to say, there are foreign firms that are doing lending business with sound practices.

Generally speaking, I am under the impression that many American and European businessmen lack sufficient knowledge of the Japanese economy, particularly that of the real estate market. I would guess many executives have no idea on how strong the rights of the tenants are in this country.

I am also suspecting that foreign executives in Japan are too lenient when evaluating the performance of those who work under them, since the performance of their Japanese staff is directly linked to the bosses' own performance and pay.

Over the coming years, many foreign companies in Japan will work furiously to raise the prices of real estate in Japan and benefit from it. At the same time, there will also be companies that quietly close their branches and leave Japan, having been disappointed at the performance of the market.

Appraisers' Roles in Asset Inflation

For those of us in the real estate appraisal industry, the creation of the asset bubble in the 1980s and early 1990s and its bursting was a very familiar problem. So we need to sincerely reflect on the past and renew our determination to prevent the recurrence of similar mistakes.

Graph 1

Rate of change in posted price and remuneration of real estate appraisal

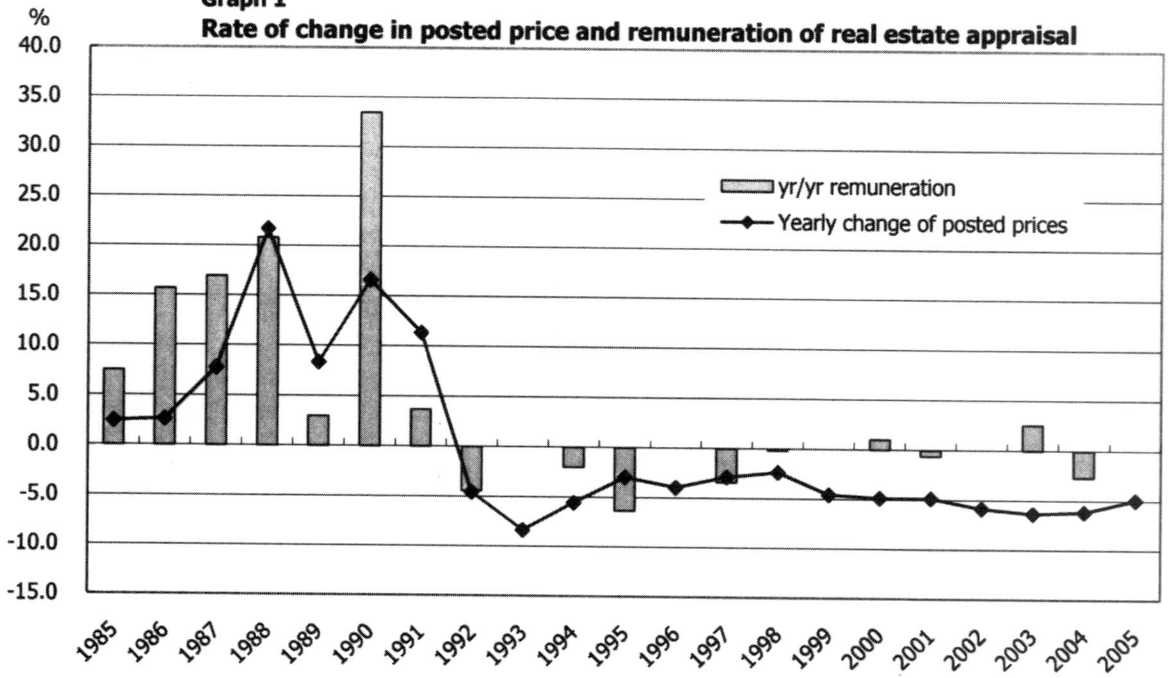

Note: 1993, 1996, 1999, 2002 and 2005 were excluded because continuity of remuneration cannot be secured since reassessment of fixed property tax was done in those years. (Data from the Ministry of Land, Infrastructure and Transport)

As part of that effort, let's examine the link between the real estate bubble and the real estate appraisal fee.

First, let's look at the trend of land prices (based on the average posted prices from 1985 to 1991) as they went up during the boom and how appraisal fees changed from year to year. (See Graph 1)

When the posted land price is on the rise, the increase in the real estate appraisal fee is much greater than the appreciation of the land price. It is very clear the land price bubble did a lot of favor to real estate appraisers.

During this period, the appraisal work was mostly done for investors who wanted to purchase real estate properties.

On the other hand, for five to six years after bursting of the bubble, starting from 1992, appraisers' fees showed declines similar to those in the posted land price. During those years, the compensation for appraisal directly reflected a drop in the number of real estate transactions. So we can say that the fall in land prices and the number of transactions affected the amount of appraisal fees.

The declining trend in appraisal fees began to level out around 1998, but land prices continued to fall. It was about that time demand for appraisal work relating to the disposal of bad loans by financial institutions exploded.

In other words, while realtors and banks were suffering from the fall in land prices, real estate appraisers were having a good time. Appraisal work related to bad loans more than offset the drop in orders from public agencies and the decline in work related to new loans.

In most cases, appraisers are brought in when a property is sold or purchased, but we do have roles outside of such transactions. People often sympathize with us for not getting enough work when the real estate business is slacking or when the prices of real estate are falling. Actually, those situations don't affect our business as much as people imagine.

I sometimes tease people by asking this question: Do appraisal requests come to us more often when land prices are rising? Or do they increase when land prices are falling? Which do you think is the case?

Land Auction and the Bubble

How did the burst of the bubble affect real estate financing? The media spent a lot of time talking about this. But most reporters just looked at symbolic cases in big cities, and I am left with the impression that no newspaper or television station put together a story that explained the issue systematically with concrete information.

Interestingly, the court is the institution that owns huge amounts of data that can tell us the real picture of the land price fall. The problem is nobody has conducted a large-scale study or looked at the data to analyze the last land price inflation. I would say very precious data are buried in the courthouse for those who really want to know the true effect of the bubble, how we should reconstruct our economy from the bubble's damage and how to prevent similar mistakes in the future.

Since 1994, Sanyu System Real Estate Finance Institute has conducted various research on auction markets under the jurisdiction of the district courts of Tokyo, Osaka, Nagoya, Yokohama, Saitama, Chiba, Kobe and Kyoto. (As mentioned before, the auction market will be dealt with in detail in chapter 6.) Why are we engaged in such a research that doesn't look related to our business? Well, there is a legitimate reason.

In newspapers from 1992 and 1993, soon after bursting of the bubble, we often found announcements made by central government ministries and financial institutions on housing loan companies. They gave detailed figures on bad loans held by these companies. At the same time, the person who made the announcement said without hesitation, "70 percent to 80 percent of bad loans are recoverable."

The reporters covering related areas tried hard to find out what the amount of bad loans were and who the borrowers were, but they didn't ask if 70 to 80 percent of the loans could really be collected as claimed by the creditors, and if so, on what ground. In fact, newspaper headlines just repeated what the creditors said and often reported, "Recovery Rate Predicted at 70 percent to 80 percent."

At that time, from the standpoint of a real estate appraiser, I was watching declining appraisal figures and the amount of mortgage issued, and I knew such a collection rate was impossible. That is because even if the price of a lot goes down, the amount of mortgage remains the same. Hoping to prepare some materials to prove this point, using auction data from the court, we started putting together the research. The data from the court was the only source available.

As we believe that the research from Sanyu System Real Estate Finance Institute is something that should be read and studied by people engaged in finance, we are making it available to the public as soon as a portion of analysis work is done. Recently, however, the mass media does not pay much attention to our research.

If you want to find out the real nature of financial institutions during the bubble era, analyze auction data, and you can really see their incredible conduct. Let's look at condominiums as an example familiar to most of us. A new condominium in Tokyo for family use probably cost around 50 million yen during the bubble era, and a studio apartment about 30 million yen. Used properties probably cost 10 percent to 30 percent cheaper.

Now, let's look at some of the properties successfully sold at auctions at the Tokyo District Court after 1994. The average size of loans using these condominiums as collaterals was between 100 million to 200 million every year. There must have been a few

Table 6
Mortgage value, highestl bid price and recovery ratio per condominium at Tokyo District Court

	Mortgage value of awarded property (million yen)	Highest bid price (million yen)	Recovery ratio
1994	172	43	25.0%
1995	149	25	16.8%
1996	160	18	11.3%
1997	183	20	10.9%
1998	180	17	9.4%
1999	139	11	7.9%
2000	185	17	9.2%
2001	198	16	8.1%
2002	143	17	11.9%
2003	119	16	13.4%
2004	108	16	14.8%

super luxurious condominiums in the batch, but the majority were family-sized or studio apartment. So if we suppose the average price of a secondhand condominium to be 40 million yen, the mortgage worth four to five times was issued on the property. (Table 6—Surveyed by Sanyu System Real Estate Finance Institute. Attribution is the same for the rest of this chapter.)

Even though it was during the time of easy credit, it is really amazing that they lent out so much money using condominiums as collaterals. Even more amazing are these loans: the actual collection rate, or the ratio of the successful tender price of a condominium against the mortgaged value.

For four consecutive years after 1994, the actual collection rate was less than 10 percent of the mortgaged amount. In 1999, the ratio was only 7.9 percent. That roughly equals one year's worth of interest on the total money lent. The momentum of the real estate price increase during the bubble was so strong that loan officers at banks probably believed the price of a condominium will be worth four to five times the current level in a few years. But looking back now, using these figures, it is not hard to see why even healthy banks got into serious trouble.

Land Alone Was Not Popular

Let's compare the collection rates for loans lent on a lot without a house on it, a lot with a house, a commercial property and a condominium as collateral. (See Table 7)

Cleared land performed the worst when it comes to the actual collection rate. You might think they will do well because it's easy to tell whether the property is unlawfully occupied by someone. And an empty lot is flexible for the new owner. But what happened was the opposite. It could be that the bank was too optimistic about these benefits and appraised the property too high and lent too much money.

The collection rate for a lot with a house on it was the highest of the four categories of the properties. Though both categories are for household use, the collection rate for houses was more than 10 percent higher than for condominiums. Commercial properties are often thought of as a difficult item for auctions since they are expensive and limited in use. But their actual collection rate was higher than condominiums.

For your information, the prices of successful bids at auctions at the Tokyo District Court in 2002, classified by the type of collateral, were 94 million yen for commercial properties, 58 million yen for empty lots, 37 million yen for house and 17 million for a condominium. I must say these levels are reasonable.

Based on the levels of successful bids, we estimate the value of properties in Osaka is less than 80 percent of that of Tokyo, Nagoya is less than 20 percent of Tokyo or a quarter of Osaka. (See Table 8)

Table 7

Recovery ratio by type of collateral at Tokyo District Court

	Land	One-unit home	Commercial property	Condominium	Total
1994	24.3%	23.2%	28.3%	25.0%	24.7%
1995	15.3%	25.6%	17.0%	16.8%	18.7%
1996	10.0%	21.9%	16.7%	11.3%	14.3%
1997	9.3%	18.8%	12.7%	10.9%	12.7%
1998	6.0%	20.0%	12.0%	9.4%	11.4%
1999	5.3%	16.2%	11.5%	7.9%	10.4%
2000	6.3%	16.7%	11.8%	9.2%	11.3%
2001	7.5%	18.9%	11.9%	8.1%	11.8%
2002	9.2%	23.0%	14.1%	11.9%	14.2%
2003	10.5%	22.3%	19.3%	13.2%	17.8%
2004	15.7%	28.3%	24.5%	14.9%	22.1%

Table 8

Highest bid price per case at Tokyo, Osaka and Nagoya District Courts (April - Sept/2006)

(million yen)

	Tokyo	Osaka	Nagoya
Land	57.0	46.6	12.0
Buildings on leased land	34.1	14.0	5.2
Buildings with land	82.0	41.9	28.5
Condominiums	19.2	12.7	10.0
Total	**43.3**	**29.6**	**17.5**

4
How the Price of Land is Determined

Different Types of Land Pri ces

Some of the readers may be thinking of buying a new home. Now it has become a common practice to bargain when buying a property. And many of you may be suspicious of the prices you see on real estate fliers, particularly if in the past you have seen a real estate agent whispering in your ear sharply discounted prices.

If an owner of real estate is desperate to sell her lot or house, the price may become lower than its market value. Conversely, if a person wants to buy a lot right next to his own out of necessity, he may be willing to pay more than its market value because it is more valuable to him than to other people. Transactions between relatives, inheritance, or auction—various reasons can be involved in buying or selling real estate. Accordingly, prices can vary. These transactions are different in nature from the stock market where much more information can be shared among participants. There it is much easier to figure out the fair value of what you have.

Does this mean that in the property market, "what was paid" in the previous transaction becomes the fair price of the property? No. It's not that simple. It is true that whenever there is a transaction, a market is created, and along with it a price. But there are exceptions. Let's look at the case of a bank using real estate as

Table 9

Comparison of official land values (Posted land prices set at 100)

	Posted land price	**Land price suveyed by municipalities (Standard land price)**	**Inheritance tax assessment (Price of land fronting major road)**	**Assessed value of fixed asset (Priceof land fronting major road)**
Who determines?	Land ministry	Prefectural authority	IRS	Local municipality
Relevant date	Every Jan. 1	Every Jul. 1	Every Jan. 1	Jan. 1 of year before base year (Every 3 years)
Publicity date	March	September	August	March
Usage	For guidance under Act for Planning the Utilization of the National Land and for land expropriation.	To complement posted price. Also for partial announcement of the same land spots as standard spots for posted prices as their standard land spots.	For calculation base of inheritance and gift taxes.	For calculation base of fixed property tax, city-planning tax, real property acquisition tax, registration and license tax.
Price level	100	100	80	70

collateral. There will be no contract for the property itself and therefore there is no price for the property.

Now, how is its price going to be determined? First of all, when we talk about land prices in Japan, we consider the price of land without a house on top. Also, the price of the land here means its unit price, measured per square meter or *tsubo,* not the entire lot.

Roughly, there are four types of official land prices. They are: the posted land price [hereafter indicated as (**a**)], the standard land price (**b**), the inheritance tax assessment, also known as the road-side price, (**c**) and the property tax assessment. (**d**). (See Table 9) These prices are needed when the central government or public organizations sell or buy land, or when they impose taxes. The reason for having all of these different types of prices is because the concept of fairness is important. Financial institutions also make use of official prices in their financing business. Outside of these four categories, there are also prices of a more private nature that are used in actual real estate transactions or by borrowers when taking out loans. We will look into these prices in detail later.

Are Official Land Prices Useful?

The posted land price (**a**) and the standard land price (**b**) are both price indicators with the same characteristics required under the Act for Planning the Utilization of the National Land. Yet, they are prepared and administered by different governing bodies; the National Land and Transportation Ministry and local prefectural governments. The number of survey spots in 2004 was 31,866 for posted prices and 27,577 for standard prices. The dates of the assessments are also different; January 1 is for the posted prices and July 1 is for the standard price. The survey spots are also different, but in recent years they are trying as much as possible to choose the same spots for both surveys. The common survey spots in 2004 were 1,199 points for housing lots and 488 for commercial lots. Thus a mesh of spots covers the entire national land. It is not practical to evaluate the entire land of Japan because that would be so time consuming and expensive. So the governments have to pick proper spots to estimate their value and publicize them. The only way to estimate their value of the entire land in Japan is to add up the property tax assessment for each tax payer.

The two different official land prices are expected to be unified in the future, and instead of making the data available once a year, they will eventually publicize them twice a year for the benefit of users.

The posted and standard land prices are shown according to how the land is used. They are classified into the area designated for urbanization (housing lots, would-be housing lots, commercial lots, quasi-industrial lots, industrial lots), non-urbanization area (housing lots, forest land), and other city planning areas (residential and commercial lots). How to choose the survey points for posted and standard prices is stipulated in the Posted Land Price Act and its enforcement regulations.

For example, Article 2 of the enforcement regulation defines the conditions for designating the posted spots and the standard spots as follows: "The spot, in a coherent area where the use of land is recognized to be identical, is a mass of land where the land use, environment, acreage, configuration, etc. are recognized to be normal in the area where the plot is located." In accordance with this rule, for the assessment of a commercial area, for example, the property has to have an area close to the average size of the land owned by shop owners in the neighborhood. The property also needs to be located in an average location, not in an outlying area or in the most central area. If most shops in the area stand on a lot with 100 *tsubo,* the survey spot needs to have roughly that size of land. If it is a small scale shopping district with small shops of 20 to 30 *tsubo* each, that will be the size of the designated land.

However, the number of evaluation spots, even putting both posted and standard spots together, is less than 60,000 in the entire country. As posted and standard spots become unified further, the figure will drop and the mesh of the spots covering the nation's land will have bigger holes. When that happens, the evaluation spot may not be located anywhere near the property sought to be appraised. Then it will become hard for the bank, buyer and seller of the property to find out the fair value for the property they are interested in.

Since the posted price and the standard price are closely related to taxation, land purchase by the government, and land administration, tend to be influenced by the government's needs each year. It is a little-known fact that posted and standard points are often altered in order to prevent the government's land price policy from being criticized, for allowing a sharp rise or fall. The continuity in the assessment method and policy is absent.

The time lag is another problem because the posted land prices are assessed as of January 1 of each year and don't become public until the end of March. By the time you want to refer to it, it could be quite obsolete. Actually, the posted land prices are put together, at the request of the national and local governments, by real estate appraisers, using information on the real estate transactions for the previous one year period. To be in time for the March announcement, appraisers collect materials at branch offices of the Legal Affairs Bureau from October to December of the previous year, and the materials collected give the information on real property transactions carried out from November of two years before to October of that year. The information available here is related to the transfer of ownership only. The information on prices is collected through questionnaires for the old and new owners of properties, as we will study later.

As posted land price, therefore, could reflect the market situation as old as two and a half years before, in the worst cases. If the user of the information uses it right after the announcement, the price obtained should be the market prices of 0.5–2.5 years before. But if the user waits until right before the following year's announcement comes out, the price data could be as old as 1.5– 2.5 years. So when the market is moving rapidly, the posted prices can be rather out of date.

The good news is the posted prices—which include ten pieces of information, including the lot numbers, residence indication, prices per square meter, acreage, and configuration—are easily available. The National Land and Transportation Ministry makes it available on the Internet free of charge. Even the price information for all spots in the country can be purchased for about 10,000 yen.

Tax Assessments Can Be Useful

Just like (**a**) and (**b**), the roadside land prices used for the purposes of inheritance tax (**c**) are made public once a year. These prices are for land facing certain roads, and require that the land lots are of standard configuration, and not of unusual shapes like a triangle or a narrow strip of land. It is stipulated the price should be such and such percent less or such and such percent more if the land is in an unusual shape or in an unusual location. This applies, for example, when a lot is particularly deep, or when it is located in a street corner.

Compared with the posted land price, the inheritance tax assessments cover the country much more thoroughly. But even these are not perfect. Some local areas still practice an evaluation method known as the "multiplier."

Evaluation by multiplier is not used where (**c**) is not available. According to the government's notice regarding the evaluation of property for inheritance tax, the calculation is to be made by multiplying the assessed value of a lot by a certain ratio. (The metropolitan tax office, ward offices, city halls, and town and village offices have all the assessed value of fixed assets.) The multiplying ratio varies depending on areas, but can be confirmed at tax offices. The area where (**c**) is not available is called "multiplication area."

(**c**) and the posted land price are similar in that they both can be affected by the government's policy reasons and that their information is old. Real estate appraisers do not seem to make much use of these prices, but they can provide useful information when they compare prices of properties at different locations.

The assessed value of properties for property-tax purposes (**d**) is revised every three years, but this is not fit for use by the third party because no one can see it unless permitted by the owner of the property in question. When appraisers receive a request for real estate appraisal, they can be in a position to know its assessed value, only after the owner submits his taxation certificate.

Although they are both real estate taxes, the inheritance tax is a national tax, whereas the fixed property tax is a local tax, and the prices of properties based on which the amount of tax is to be calculated are also different.

Economically, I think Japan is almost a socialist country in that graduate taxation on income as well as hefty inheritance taxes have helped to equalize the distribution of private assets. Given this, wouldn't it be a good idea to disclose the land assessments for property tax? If it was done, those who want information on the actual price for a particular lot can deduct the price from which the property tax is calculated as the price of the lot. Then, there will be no need to compile other official prices, and the government can reduce its budget. Financial institutions would not have to spend extra money for real estate appraisal.

At any rate, there are different official prices (**a** through **d**) for the same spot of land at present. These prices sometimes vary significantly from each other, sometimes as much as 100 percent.

Incidentally, in obtaining assessments for property tax, the price of a building and its useful life can be taken into consideration, but the rules here also vary depending on the materials used. Also, the property that is very unique or very particular; for example a house with few but very large rooms, will not easily be transacted when one wants to sell it and consequently becomes less expensive than a typical building of the same size.

Real Estate Appraisers and the Posted Prices

Now, let's examine who decides posted prices. At the request of the national and local governments, commercial real estate appraisers are the ones to do the job. This is in accordance with the Real Estate Appraisal Law.

Since the posted land price law took effect on July 1, 1969, appraisers have been involved in determining land prices. By that time, the system of appraisers had been fully established, and the demand had been rising for real estate appraisal as back-up materials for business transactions.

This law allows the appraisers in charge of the task to visit satellite offices of the district legal affairs bureau, and check, for free of charge, the status of the ownership of the properties either sold or bought during the previous year.

Real estate appraisers conduct a survey by sending out questionnaires to both new and previous owners of the properties whose registers show ownership changes, which generally mean that there had been transactions. Completed questionnaires are to be sent to Japan Association of Real Estate Appraisal. (The membership consists of real estate appraisal companies, individual appraisers and assistant appraisers. See chapter 5. Unlike lawyers, however, appraisers can practice without becoming members of this organization.) In Tokyo, typically 10 percent of the questionnaires sent out are filled in and returned.

The Introduction to the questionnaire sent to sellers and buyers in the name of the Japan Association of Real Estate Appraisal and Tokyo Association of Real Estate Appraisers reads as follows:

Re: Questions regarding your land transaction.

Dear Sirs and Madams,

We, the Japan Association of Real Estate Appraisal and the Tokyo Association of Real Estate Appraisers, have been conducting a survey on land price posting, land price research and land price trend. We also study land transactions, at the request of the national government and Tokyo metropolitan government.

Posted land prices and standard land prices obtained as a result of these surveys are made public every year by both the national government and municipal governments. These data are widely used as references when people try to sell or purchase real estate or when they want to know the levels of the market and price trend in Tokyo.

In order to make these surveys as accurate as possible, it is indispensable that we gather as many samples of land transactions as possible. The information that you provide will be very valuable for us in order to understand appropriate price levels and price trend in our day-to-day appraisal work.

We would appreciate it very much if you could understand our goal and fill in and return the separate survey sheet regarding your latest transaction. We would like to call your attention to Article 38 of Real Estate Appraisal Law, which require us to keep the information strictly confidential. We will do everything possible for the safe administration of all the information that you provide.

The items on the land and building transaction survey sheet are as follows:

1. Location (lot number)
2. Location (address)
3. The segmentation of ownership, leasehold, and land-lease income rights
4. The presence or absence of a building
5. Contract date
6. Date of application for register
7. Name of the seller (a private individual or corporation)
8. Name of the buyer (private individual or corporation)
9. The total value of the transaction for the land and/or building, measured per square meter
10. Lot space on register and actual measurements, the size of private pathway if any, and configuration of lot
11. Category of building, size, structure, number of stories, date of construction
12. Circumstances for transaction

Based on the response to these questions, appraisers conduct on-the-spot examination of posted points and transaction points and create case cards for actual transactions. Finally, two appraisers determine the posted price of each point. At the same time, local appraisal associations decide the price of each posted point in its area. When prefectures conduct price surveys, each point is assessed by one appraiser.

Who Owns the Case Cards?

Without transaction case cards, appraisers cannot prepare accurate appraisal reports quickly. The issue of who controls the cards—who are allowed to see them or how much to charge for browsing them—have been left to each prefectural association for real estate appraisal.

Most associations let member appraisers browse through or make copies of their cards for relatively low fees. But since they worked so hard to compile these cards, some associations do not allow outsiders to see them, or charge higher fees for viewing or copying them.

The purpose of these fees isn't making money. Rather, they are charged to discourage people from reading them. The appraisers don't want to share the information with lots of other people.

But come to think of it, who really owns these information materials and who can make use of them? Here are the typical views of experts.

1. The information materials that have been gathered by national or prefectural governments for the purpose of determining posted or standard land prices should belong to those governments.
2. They should belong to real estate appraisers and real estate appraisal associations that actually gathered and processed the data.
3. The materials were collected with the consent from those who sold or bought real estate. Their purpose was to determine posted or other official land prices. So the data should belong to those who actually filled in the questionnaires, or the people who had bought or sold properties.
4. The legal affairs bureau that gives permission to appraisers to see the status of the ownership should have

the right to the data. Any use other than for computing posted and standard land prices should be banned.

From April 1, 2005, the personal information protection law will be enforced, so this also has to be brought into consideration. Because the transaction case cards held by the real estate appraisal associations include such highly personal information as the names of buyers and sellers, types of their transactions, timing and value. Even though the access to these cards is limited to appraisers, isn't there any problem in letting strangers have such information?

Probably someday, the practice of letting only appraisers see transaction cards will become obsolete. As I will mention later, even at present, a group of realtors under the jurisdiction of the National Land and Transportation Ministry has set up across the nation organizations with such names as "The Real Estate Information Network for East Japan" and "Real estate Information Network for Osaka Metropolitan District" (known as REINS). These groups offer firsthand information on property transactions to their members. Sanyu System's affiliate, TAS, also makes available to the public each appraisal case after making standardizing adjustments. Needless to say, by buying housing information magazines, anybody can easily see the prices at which owners want to sell their properties.

Furthermore, the national land ministry is considering having people report the prices of land lots, condominiums and office buildings at the time of registration and making them available on the Internet. The information to be made public will include, in the case of a land lot, its approximate location, land category, date of the transaction, and transaction price.

The ministry was initially planning to make this mandatory under law, but now it seems to be thinking of making it a voluntary system, and hoping that people will cooperate.

The total number of annual real estate transactions in Japan is, on average, 1.6 million, including commercial buildings, independent houses, condominiums and other properties, both new and used. If the land ministry's idea is materialized, it would be an epoch-making event, and the roles of real estate appraisers and real estate agents should change drastically.

Appraisal Fees for Public Prices

One may wonder why real estate appraisers who are not public officials are involved in public decisions at all. It is because the government does not have the expertise and personnel for determining land prices. So private real estate appraisal companies are mobilized. In this sense, real estate appraisal firms may come under the same category as Japan Railways, Nippon Telephone and Telegraph, security companies (the police), and staffing companies (the Public Employment Security Office) in that they assist the work of the government. So it is perceivable that a real estate appraisal company could grow into such a big and important company, similar to one of those former state-owned enterprises. Such a company would be given a mandate to compute posted prices on behalf of the government.

For example, the national land ministry mobilizes real estate appraisers once a year to evaluate 31,866 spots across the country and make posted prices public. But those who make use of the information want more spots to be evaluated, or when price fluctuation is big, they think surveys should be conducted not just once but four times a year.

So, it is possible that in the future, the government will give up compiling the posted prices and leave it to the private sector. Instead of publicly announced land prices, data compiled by various private companies can serve the purpose for interested people. One company's prices may cover 10,000 locations but be announced just once a year. Another company, meanwhile, may

• Official announcement of land prices	46.9 billion yen	31,866 spots	Ministry of Land, Infrastructure and Transport
• Survey on land price trend for a six-month period	19.5 billion yen	2,675 spots	(Started in 2004)
• Prefectural land price survey	21.6 billion	27,725 spots	Each prefectural government **Half of this had been subsidized by the central government until 2003.*
• Roadside land prices for inheritance tax computation	13.6 billion yen	18,450 spots	Ministry of Finance
• Roadside land prices for property tax computation	25.0 billion yen	420,000 spots	Municipal Government **The above figures were prepared by the Ministry of Internal Affairs and Communications for answering questions raised at the parliament. The number of overlapping spots is approximately 30,000.*

limit the areas of coverage to just three major metropolitan areas but update its information every month. If some of these indicators receive the official seal of approval, the users can pick the one that suits their needs the best.

In any case, the current system of official land prices, where four different price indicators are announced by different ministries is wasteful. It uses enormous amounts of budget, but all it does is to show different prices for the same spots. For your information, the 2003 budgets appropriated for land appraisal by the central government, prefectural governments, and municipal governments are shown on page 85.

The money allocated under these budgets is used primarily to pay outside contractors such as real estate appraisers. It does not include personnel costs and other expenses of administrative offices of the government.

So instead of conducting surveys on multiple levels, the government should use just one survey, and set different multipliers for different purposes. For example, the assessment for the same spot can be lowered if it's used for tax purposes.

Various Private Prices

When banks lend money on real estate as collateral, they must first know the total market value of the property, and then offer a loan up to a certain percentage of that value. If the value of the property can be obtained through official data, no property appraisal is necessary.

But as I have mentioned before there would be several problems with such a system. 1) You might know the standard price in the area in question, but you don't know the value of the particular property you are interested in. 2) The data could be obsolete, depending on when you make use of the price information; if you are using the data just before the following year's announcement is made, the prices could be as many as two and a half years old. Therefore you cannot utilize these prices when the market is moving rapidly. 3) The roadside land price for the property tax purpose is the price the government determines for the property. But unless the owner discloses the figure, it doesn't become public. The government cannot disclose the prices to the third party because of confidentiality rules.

These problems aren't acceptable to financial institutions. If the banks ask government organizations to appraise the value of the properties they are interested in, these organizations would decline because they think they are not supposed to do such work. Besides they are not capable of doing the job and do not have human resources to do it either.

So, the banks have no choice but to do the appraisal work for themselves or to ask private appraisal companies to evaluate the properties. Thus, private prices, as opposed to government-posted prices, become essential.

Private prices include: 1) one that a party concerned wishes to use when setting the buying or selling price of the property ("the seller's price/buyer's price"), 2) the price at which the transaction was actually closed (the real estate transaction price), 3) the price obtained by an appraiser for a particular property at a particular time (the real estate appraisal value), and 4) a standard price for a standard property in a particular area evaluated by an appraiser (the standard appraisal value).

Subjective Prices That Sellers Want

Let's look at the item 1) mentioned above; the seller's price and the buyer's price almost never reflect the real market trend. Those prices are put together, reflecting the owner's wish to make a lot of money, or the buyer's hope to limit his exposure. It could be a price that the seller calculates back from the value of the item he wants to buy with the proceeds from the sale of the property. Or it could be based on the amount of the debt that the seller needs to pay back once the property is sold. In other words, those prices have little objectivity, and therefore are irresponsible prices.

Prices that sellers want for their properties are listed in housing magazines piled high in bookstores. But you'll notice even for the same property, the price can vary depending on when the magazines are issued. They might ask for 100 million yen when their properties are first put on the market. But after a couple of weeks, if they remain unsold, they often reduce the price to, say, 80 million. Because the time difference is so small, the same magazine may carry two different prices for the same property. Which price would the banks consider the right one?

To tell the truth, there can be three different kinds of sales contracts for one property; one with a price inflated for the purpose of receiving a mortgage, one with a price estimated lower for submitting to the tax office and one that reflects the real value. The buyer and the seller can produce many pieces of evidence for their transactions.

Here is a story we often heard during the bubble economy. It may sound like a joke, but it is a true story. In order to secure a bigger mortgage, a real estate buyer, in conspiracy with a real estate agent, makes up and add for a housing magazine which lists the property at two or three times its real value. The property buyer and the agent visit a bank and show the magazine to give the banker an impression that the real estate is being transacted at a high price. Thus they succeed in wangling the bank into lending to the seller a large sum of money.

Having had a bitter experience of being misled by these fake land prices, large banks have begun to do their own research so that they won't have to depend on housing magazines anymore. But unfortunately there still are some financial institutions that rely on the price information carried in these magazines.

Transaction Prices are Hard to Get

Actual transaction prices mentioned under the item 2) cannot be known to people other than the sellers, buyers, real estate agents and the tax offices. Except for the questionnaire sent out by the government to determine the posted land prices, they will not be gathered in an organized way. If examples of actual transactions are needed, you will have to work hard and be patient in gathering the information. At present, even such private organizations that keep case examples, such as REINS have to obtain transaction prices as a favor from the parties involved in transactions, or buy such information from brokers. For that type of information, though, there is no way for the third party to confirm whether it is accurate or not. That's because you have no way to confirm the real price mentioned in the contract. If you really want to know, you will have to visit the parties involved in the transaction and ask point blank. Naturally, the cost of gathering such information will be higher. The users of the information should check it against a certified copy of the register to make sure the transaction did actually take place. But are they really doing such work?

As to item 3, before a seller sells his property, or before a buyer purchases it, before a bank lends money, or when they want to know the going price during the period of lending, people want to know the property's appraisal value and they will normally ask an appraisal company to get it for them. But the appraisal prices cannot be made available to the outsiders because the appraisers who did the job are obligated to keep the results confidential.

Item 4, the standard appraisal value is an industry jargon. It is the price worked out by an appraiser, envisioning an average property in the area where the property in question exists. An average property means a property that has the same value as other average properties, after eliminating the uniqueness of each individual property.

For example, if most subsections are 500 *tsubo* each in a certain industrial area, then a land lot for industrial use with an area of about 500 *tsubo* is a standard property in the area. And if most roads are five meters wide, a lot facing a five-meter road is a standard property. On the other hand, a luxurious private house in an industrial zone had a different intended use, and an attempt to build a similar house will unlikely be permitted, and therefore cannot be a standard property there.

The Problems with Transaction Prices

Actual transaction prices and standard appraisal values are what banks and real estate appraisers might refer to when they want to know the price of a property. When we compare those two different values, generally speaking, transaction prices are the accurate prices at which the properties were actually sold and bought. On the other hand, standard appraisal values are academic prices that have little to do with real transactions and tend to be made light of. But that perception is wrong for the reasons mentioned below.

First, transaction prices may not be accurate. As mentioned previously, the prices that parties involved in transaction and real estate agents disclose are not always right. The tax office wouldn't tell them even if they knew. Even whether there really was a transaction isn't clear.

Secondly, sellers often refer to the total value of their real estate, including both the land and the building. So when a seller says, for example, "I sold the house for 100 million yen," the amount covers both the land and the house. The prices you often see are the total amounts, without specifying how much the land was worth and how much the building was.

In this case, in order to know the unit price of the land, you must first divide the total price into the price of the lot and that of the building. But it cannot easily be done. It will be necessary to do an on-the-spot survey. It will take time and money which is probably no less than what it cost to calculate an appraisal price.

Thirdly, the prices they obtained reflect all kinds of peculiar situations that arise at the time of transactions, regarding the land, areas, and circumstances the buyer and seller were in. Without standardizing a process, the prices that include these special elements are being utilized.

Peculiarity can include the following five elements: 1) the circumstances of buyers and sellers, 2) the timing of the transaction, 3) the extent of effective utilization of the land in relation to the building, 4) other individual contributing factors such as the shape of the lot, or the type of the road which the lot faces, and 5) regional difference in the prices.

As for the circumstances of the buyers and sellers, for instance, a person may want to sell her lot quickly as she is being transferred to another city. It could involve a seller who is willing to accept a lower price in order to close the deal at a certain point of time in order to make some tax savings. A property involved in an unpleasant incident often falls in price. On the contrary, the next-door neighbor of a property on sale may be willing to pay more than the market price because it offers a special value for him. He may be looking for a property for his parents, who could easily show up for hot meals at the family table.

And finally, even if you somehow find out the total value of a property, you need to double-check the area of the lot if you want to know its unit price because the area given in the register can be inaccurate because measurement could have been sloppy. Whether the straw rope was slack or strained when the measurement was taken, could affect the measurement of the property. This is often the case with farmland and forestland. Therefore, it is important to check when the measurement was taken, and whether a map of the lot is available. Also in relation to the map you should check the location of the boundary stones. Needless to say, real estate appraisers do all this work in their appraisal work.

There are other numerous factors that affect land prices. To name a few, whether the land includes a private road (a private road is usually priced at 0 percent to 30 percent of the price of the adjacent land), the configuration of the lot, what kind of road it faces, whether it may be included in an area to be bought out by the government in the future, how attractive the surrounding area is, and so forth.

All these special factors contribute to the formation of the price of a property. But the way those transaction prices are described is usually rather simple. "A 100-*tsubo* located at the following address, offered at 100 million yen. Thus, the unit price per *tsubo* is 1 million yen." If you simply believe what it says and conclude that the price of a 10-*tsubo* lot located next to that lot is 10 million yen, you will be making a big mistake. That's because a lot of only 10 *tsubo* is so small that it could be of little use in certain areas.

You should not try to calculate the price of a property based on the price of an unprocessed "raw" transaction in the past. Experienced real estate appraisers are very much aware of the following rules when they look at "raw" transactions done in the past: Even if it looks fresh, uncooked food can be rotten or can carry worms inside. Here is another one: If you want to eat *sashimi* in a foreign country, you really should choose your restaurant carefully.

Foreigners Pay Excessive Attention to Transaction Prices

But many of the people in charge of appraisal at real estate agencies and financial institutions do not seem to know these rules. If they are Japanese bankers, they usually understand what I say. But things have changed in recent years as a lot of foreign financial institutions have expanded into this country. Foreign banks place too much emphasis on "raw transaction prices" and tend to spend a lot of time looking for data on past transactions. But it is doubtful whether they are processing such information into truly usable information materials.

Do they really have staff capable of visiting the places that only come with "raw" transaction data and check all the special circumstances surrounding the property? The answer is probably no. Foreign banks tend to value speed, and they tend to focus on information on "raw" transactions made available from appraisers. This blind trust in transaction prices seems to be very common among foreigners working in Japan, particularly Americans, rather than among Japanese staff working for foreign financial institutions. They are probably not aware that the quantity and quality of transaction data, and the way they are obtained here are quite different from those in the United States. I'm sorry to say this but the information in Japan is incomparably poorer than that in the U.S. In Japan, the tax authorities have access to accurate information on real estate transactions, but their data are not made public. The Japan Real estate Appraisal Association keeps some transaction prices, but they account for only 10 percent to 20 percent of the total transactions done in the country. In addition, this information is available only to appraisers who pay fees to the Association. I wouldn't say these data are useless, but compared with those in the U.S., their utility value is low.

Standardized Appraisal Value Should Be Reconsidered

Now, let's talk about the standardized appraisal prices that I briefly mentioned before. These are the prices compiled after real estate appraisers have made standardized corrections to "raw" transaction prices. They are theoretically the most reasonable and standard prices figured out by appraisers after eliminating from transaction prices all the specificity accompanying the property, such as the characteristics of the neighborhood, the features of the property itself, the demography in the surrounding area, and possibly special circumstances with the buyer or the seller. The standardized appraisal value has to be worked out in the process of appraising a specific property. Therefore, for real estate appraisers, there is no cost involved in obtaining price information. It is for this reason that I think it is not reasonable to make light of these prices, just because they are not actual transaction prices.

There is nothing strange about a buyer paying 200 million yen for a property whose appraised value was 100 million yen. In this case, because of various special elements involved, the transaction price rose to 200 million yen. Land prices are different in nature from stocks bought and sold on the stock market. Are there any appraisers who can come up with an objective price incorporating the desire of a buyer who wants to buy a lot next to his own house? It is not the same as stock analysts studying the trend of official discount rates in predicting stock prices.

Meanwhile, the standardized appraisal value can be used as it is, unlike "actual transaction prices." For example, let's say the transaction price in the target area is 100,000 yen per *tsubo,* based on data from actual transactions. When you actually visit the site, you may find the property is more conveniently located in terms of transportation than other standard lots in the area. So, if a transaction price is 10 percent higher than ordinary prices, the prices of the "standardized lot" should be made 10 percent less than actual transaction prices and lower its standardized assessment to 90,000 yen per *tsubo.* As you can see, with actual transaction prices, errors can often be made.

If, however, you knew the standardized appraisal value was 90,000 yen per *tsubo*, objective prices for the properties in the area can easily be deducted, and mistakes can also be prevented.

If the standardized appraisal value is compared to "cooked fish," actual transaction prices are "raw fish."

For many years, I have not regarded the standardized appraisal value as a by-product of a real estate appraisal survey on a specific property. Rather, I intended to make two products, namely "real estate appraisal value" and "standardized appraisal value" for appraising real estate. Other than making use of the information that comes out of our appraisal work on individual properties, Sanyu System is making a secondary use of the information by selling it to TAS Corporation and Nissei Basic Research Institute. TAS was founded as a computer technology company within the Toyota Motor group, and publishes 50,000 pieces of standardized appraisal information obtained by Sanyu each year. Nissei, meanwhile, publishes privately posted real estate prices four times a year. The standardized appraisal value makes up for all the shortcomings of actual transaction prices, and therefore in the near future I believe it will become a mainstream pricing mechanism.

Imported Appraisal Method

The theory of real estate appraisal was brought into Japan from the United States after World War II. It is almost an exact copy of the American method. For appraising the value of a property, there are basically three methods: 1) the cost approach, 2) the comparative transaction approach and 3) the profit reduction approach. It is up to the appraiser to decide which of the three methods is more important. Until about a decade ago, the comparative transaction approach had been used the most. But as the number of foreign clients increased, the profit reduction approach has become more common.

According to the real estate appraisal standard (chapter 7, section 1) issued by the Land and Transportation Ministry, the cost approach (1) is defined as a method of obtaining an estimated price of the target property, after accounting for the depreciation cost of the property. In other words, under this method, you try to obtain the price of real estate as follows: You first figure out how much it would cost to build the structure in question now. But the property was built so many years ago that its value, after depreciation, is much lower. So, generally speaking, in an urban area, the replacement value for a lot is meaningless unless such preparation costs as land filling and land formation are involved. The comparative transaction approach (2) requires you to choose appropriate sample cases out of a large number of cases collected, then make adjustments taking into consideration different circumstances (proximity to transportation, what kind of road it faces, configuration of the land, etc.), and timing (the trend of land prices after the transaction). You are also required to compare and consider the prices obtained after making comparison of area factors and individual factors, before reaching the target property's estimated price (comparative price). That is to say, you gather as many sample cases of transaction as possible, pick out what you think are appropriate and make some corrections to them. During the bubble period, profitability was not emphasized so much, and this method was often used in working out real estate prices.

Under the profit reduction method (3), you obtain the estimated value of the target property by getting the aggregate of the current value of the income the property is expected to produce in the future. In short, you figure out how much money the property in question can earn in the future, for example, in the form of rent, and following a certain calculation formula, it is then reduced to the current value to determine the value of the property in question.

Contradiction of the Profit Reduction Approach

This calculation method comprises "the direct reduction method" (on condition that the property is to be owned for good) and the "DCF method" (the property is a target of investment for a certain period of time, so the income from the property while it is owned as well as the estimated profit from selling it are both considered). What is important here is how high you set the yield that the property is expected to earn.

The three approaches for real estate appraisal were all imported from the Untied States, and they are covered by questions asked in the test that Japan's appraisers must pass to be licensed. Although appraisers are supposed to be well-versed in the three approaches, until about ten years ago, the comparative transaction approach had been used mainly, and the other two methods were hardly used. The reason usually cited was that the cost approach and profit reduction approach were "not appropriate for the property in question."

There is a reason why appraisers prefer the comparative transaction approach over the profit reduction approach. The transaction prices to be used in the comparative transaction method are, though not great in number, available at the Real Estate Appraisal Association. On the other hand, there is no organization that has comprehensive data on rent and income from properties. This is because building owners do everything they can to keep their rent information secret. Once the rent of one tenant is made public, there is a good chance that other tenants paying higher rents would start complaining.

It is for this reason that the Real Estate Appraisal Association could not gather information on rent, and appraisers, even though they were aware of the importance of the profit reduction approach, seem to have avoided the trouble of collecting sample rents for each appraisal work. In the past, they could get by just fine with the comparative transaction approach.

Conversely, financial institutions in the United States did not think much of the comparative transaction approach, and have more or less stuck to the profit reduction method and evaluation by discount ratio. This is quite understandable given that in Western countries, particularly in the United States, profits on real estate investments are closely related to the returns from other investment packages, such as government bonds, corporate bonds and savings accounts.

But in Japan, real estate investment is regarded as a totally different type of investment from other financial products. In Japan, real estate investment has its own trend, and is not so much related to the movements of other investment products. So it makes sense to consider real estate as a totally unique investment. Many Western investors do not seem to understand this point very well.

Yields That Depend on the Intention of Clients

The indicators used for the profit reduction approach are: 1) the income for the investment period, 2) the yield, and 3) the estimated price at which property will be sold in future. The information on the income (1), which is the same thing as the rent, is not easy to gather for appraisers, but not entirely impossible. In Japan, however, it is extremely difficult to determine the level of yield on real estate investments (2). One way to determine the yield will be to compare it with other assets for investment. Another approach is to compare it with levels in the past, or those in other countries. Other financial assets include government bonds, corporate bonds, and time deposits. The basis for the returns for these products is the official discount rate set by the central bank.

But after the Plaza Accord in 1985, as mentioned in chapter 3, the official discount rate has become a tool to bail out troubled financial institutions, and for a long time, it has hovered just above zero. As a result, interest rates on financial products have also been dragged down to extremely low levels. Thus they have lost correlations to real estate investment yields. We can no longer say that the return on real estate rate is such and such points above or below the government bond yield.

There is also a limit to follow real estate yields through time. Because of the zero interests rate policy, real estate returns have lost link to the official discount rate. In addition, because of the downturn in property value has continued for such a long time, we can no longer determine appropriate real estate investment yields based on their past performance.

International comparison also has a problem. To be sure, real estate markets are now being integrated into a global market, where investors go after attractive properties beyond national borders. Nevertheless, real estate appraisers have never done comparison beyond their national borders, so they are not equipped to compare the prices in, say New York, to those in Tokyo. It is, of course, the same for Hong Kong or Paris. Since there are so many restrictions on real estate transactions in Japan, it is impossible to come up with a yield comparison that satisfies all investors.

Then how do the appraisers determine the yields?

Let me tell you frankly. They are simply throwing out some numbers that they think will make the executives at foreign financial institutions happy. There are two ways to satisfy the big bosses at foreign banks. One is to make the yield about the same as those in the United States. This way, their New York headquarters will easily approve the price written on the appraisal report. This is not international comparison. The appraiser is just trying to make the price look reasonable for the American investors. They are ignoring all other elements that they are supposed to consider. We can't call this an appropriate price.

The other way is to ask how much they would like the appraisal value to be and calculate back to get the yield. "The answer is known before you solve a problem." That's exactly what they are doing.

And let me be a bit cynical. The idea of estimated selling prices for the future, as we discussed under (3), is just fascinating. In order to appraise the current value of the property, you use the predicted selling price in the future. For an incompetent and naïve person like me, this theory is beyond my grasp. If you can predict a selling price for the future, you should be able to determine the current price much more easily. In Japan, there are more than 5,000 appraisers who have passed the test that includes questions on this method. I wonder if any of them thought it made sense. I would very much like to see what their answers were in the appraiser's test.

But finally, there is a ray of hope for real estate appraisers who want to try this approach. As real estate investment trusts, or REITs, become popular in Japan, and different types of real estate investment pools go into circulation, it will be possible to derive theoretical yields based on these products. The yields on REITs are calculated using dividends and the current value of their assets. They will help appraisers come up with theoretical yields that they can use to evaluate individual properties.

5

Who are Real Estate Appraisers?

Background

The professional code for real estate appraisers states: "Actual transaction prices for real estate properties are usually determined on a case-by-case basis, and are affected by individual circumstances. Therefore, it is very difficult for ordinary people to grasp the appropriate price for a property, based on such transactions. So, in order to find appropriate prices for properties, appraisal work by professional appraisers becomes necessary" (chapter 1, section 2).

When a real estate property is to be transacted or when financial institutions lend money (or after the end of the bubble era, when loans became sour), evaluation by someone other than the people directly involved in the deal becomes necessary. Real estate appraisers are called in such circumstances.

Real estate appraisal dates back to 1897, when Nippon Kangyo Bank, the predecessor of Japan Real Estate Institute (the bank's appraisal department was succeeded by the Institute) instituted in 1897 the regulation for appraising mortgaged property. (From the book *The 20-Year History of Japan Real Estate Appraisal Association.*)

Corporate appraisers include the Japan Real Estate Association (the current organization was established in 1959), Tokyo Tatemono Co., Ltd. (founded in 1896), and Tokyo Shintaku Co.,

Ltd. (currently Nihon Fudosan Co., Ltd.). Lending money using real estate as collateral was rare until the 1930s, so the act of appraising property itself was not so common in those days.

Even during the post-war years, appraisal was done mostly when public properties were sold or bought, or when financial institutions lent money to companies. But the target was just big properties, and the use of appraisers' service was rather limited.

From the beginning, when professional real estate agents engaged in property transaction, both the buyers and sellers did not place much emphasis on the appraised value of the properties because it was the parties concerned that decided the prices. Many people thought theoretical prices worked out by third-party experts were useless. Meanwhile, appraisers themselves did not arm themselves with enough knowledge and vigor to confront real estate agents, when necessary. If the real estate agent laughs at the theoretical price of a property that the appraiser had submitted, he would turn around and retreat quietly. Accordingly, the only occasion that a real estate appraisal certificate was needed was when a public property was transacted, as it always required a judgment by an uninterested party.

But when a financial institution lent money on real estate as collateral, the parties involved, both the lender and the borrower, often have little knowledge of real estate prices. Or if only one side has knowledge of real estate, it won't be fair. So, an evaluation by a neutral person becomes necessary. In the background was a change in the social trend, and not only corporations but also private individuals started borrowing money from banks to build their homes. During the period between 1965 and 1975, a large amount of appraisal work started coming from banks. Sanyu System was established in 1980 to meet this increasing demand, and has expanded its business by dealing only with financial institutions.

Rain or Shine

The truth of the matter is that those who have heard the terms "real estate appraisal business" or "real estate appraiser" do not really know what kind of business it is. So, it is not surprising most people have no idea what appraisal means, who to ask if they need the service of an appraiser or where to find the office of an appraiser.

The law concerning real estate appraisal stipulates that the real estate appraiser is a person who is registered with the Land and Transportation Ministry or the local government and engages in evaluating real estate properties at the request of others who pay for their service.

Real estate appraisal business can be carried out either by a private individual or by a company, but each office must have a full-time appraiser. The full-time appraiser is, of course, a certified real estate appraiser but cannot work for two or more offices at the same time.

Private appraisers who constitute the majority of those engaged in this business often play triple roles—a real estate appraisal business, a full-time real estate appraiser and a real estate appraiser.

Now, in order to appraise a real estate property and determine its price, an appraiser has to visit at least four sites for the examination.

1. The site of the property to be appraised.
2. A branch or a satellite office of the District Legal Affairs Bureau.
3. The city hall or ward office.
4. A real estate agent in the area where the property is located.

On the site of the property, the appraiser determines how the property itself looks and at the same time checks out its surroundings. At the branch office of the legal affairs bureau, he must obtain a copy of the registration for the property, an official map, a drawing of a building, and etc., and check them against the property in question. At the city hall or ward office, he checks the local zoning and city planning rules, and determines which area the property is located. And finally, the appraiser visits a local real estate agent and gathers at least three cases of recent property transactions to use as the base of their evaluation of the property.

When the real estate appraisal system was instituted, information on real estate transactions was not available at one place, and appraisers were obliged to visit local realtors one by one and ask for transaction prices. It was a tough part of their job as it required much time and effort. Fortunately, as I mentioned in chapter 4, since appraisers came to be involved in determining posted prices, the local office of the Real Estate Appraisal Association started collecting case cards for past transactions. Now the appraisers just need to visit these offices.

Thus, appraisers visit four different places for appraisal of a single property. It may not sound so hard, but depending on which time of the year it is, this could be a difficult task.

Visiting a site during the summer can be a hard physical work. You need to take a water bottle. If the place is not accessible by car, you will have to walk. Sometimes you need to wear boots to prevent snake bites.

The snow season is another tough time. You could fall on ice and break your bones. And caution must be used when you evaluate a snow-covered lot. An appraiser who is not familiar with the area visits a site and may conclude that the property is flat and is suitable for residential or factory use. The price will be determined accordingly. When the spring comes and the snow melts, she may find there is a pond on the site. You may not believe it, but this is a true story. I wonder what exactly the appraiser told her client when she went to apologize.

At our company, we pay extra attention to appraisal work in

winter. It is not a concern in Tokyo, but in snowy areas, you cannot even visit a site during the winter.

When examining a property, appraisers peek through the windows of the house or step into the yard, or take pictures of the entrance as if such conducts are permitted. Not surprisingly, they are sometimes mistaken for a sneak thief or a prowler. Particularly troublesome is when a young man is trying to borrow money on the house as collateral from a consumer finance company without telling his parents. The parents see an appraiser prowling around their house, and ask what on earth he was doing. They find out what's going on and have a big fight with the son. Then the son might rush to the bank and make a violent protest.

Properties that are foreclosed as the borrowers become insolvent present problems sometimes. At least once a year or so, you hear about an appraiser who mopes around a foreclosed property to make a report for the creditor, and gets caught by the debtor. Then the appraiser's office calls up the creditor, and begs them to rush to the debtor's place and have the appraiser released.

Visiting a golf course on the brink of bankruptcy is another headache. If you keep taking pictures without playing golf, players might complain you are violating their privacy. Or they could suspect the golf course is about to go bankrupt. So in order to avoid a possible trouble like that, you play a game and quickly take pictures pretending you are taking shots of your company.

After all this hardship, you come out with an appraised value, but if it is to the client's disadvantage, he might give you a bitter complaint. This is a profession full of tears and laughter.

How to Become a Real Estate Appraiser

In order to become a fully-licensed real estate appraiser, you must pass three sets of tests. One step before that is an "assistant appraiser." If you pass the second test and have more than two years of experience working on real estate appraisal, you are eligible for it. Just passing the second test is not enough. Unless you actually work under an appraiser for over two years, you cannot be an assistant real estate appraiser.

Furthermore, real estate appraisers and assistant appraisers are not supposed to claim those titles unless you register with the Land and Transportation Ministry.

The real estate appraisal law was enacted in 1963. Prior to that, such organizations as the Japan Real Estate Institute and other trust companies offered appraisal services, but only to a limited number of special users. Let us look at the history of the real estate appraisal examination from a page from *The 20-Year History of Japan Real Estate Appraisal Association.*

> After the first special test in 1964 and through a concomitant use of special and common tests in 1965 and 1966, we started using the current system in 1967, giving the first, second and third tests. (The first test is to see if the examinee has the academic ability equal to that of a university graduate, the second test is for the qualification as an assistant real estate appraiser, and the third test is for becoming a fully-licensed real estate appraiser.)
>
> In 1970, the land price posting system was introduced, boosting the demand for regional appraisers. Also in the same year, a bill sponsored by lawmakers was passed. It was called "the law on real estate appraiser's preferential tests and assistant real estate appraiser's preferential tests." Those tests were conducted only twice, in 1970 and 1971.
>
> Also, as a preferential measure due to the return of Okinawa to Japan, special tests for appraisers in Okinawa were given three times from 1972 through 1974. Those who passed the special and preferential tests were called "preferential appraisers."

And for twenty years thereafter, they cultivated strong ties with local bureaucrats, dominated the appraisal business and had a strong impact on the history of the appraisal industry.

The Industry Controlled by Veteran Appraisers

There were two reasons why the appraisers who passed the special and preferential tests have had such strong influence in the industry.

One of the reasons is the system under which those who passed the second test are qualified for taking the third test only after working for more than two years under real estate appraisers.

Candidates for the third test must get a signature from the real estate appraiser under whom they completed the practical training. Seeing this system from an educational point of view, it is a good system because a student can study face to face with the teacher using a property that really exists as a learning material. That's why the system is still working. But while successful candidates are receiving practical training, the teacher-student relationship changes into a boss-henchman relationship. A kind of apprentice system is created.

It has long been a custom to hire a candidate with no pay or a very small salary after offsetting the tuition for training with the candidate's pay during the period of practical training. Thus, the appraiser who was in the position of teacher could use the candidate for on-the-spot survey of sites or writing appraisal reports at little or no cost for more than two years. They could run their office without personnel costs.

There was a joke that the teacher made the student write so many appraisal reports that he became unable to write any without the student.

Another reason is the fact that those veteran appraisers had excellent sales capabilities. In those days, most appraisal requests came from the government and local municipalities, and there was not a conspicuous increase or decrease in the number of new clients. Properties to be appraised were almost of the same type every year. All appraisers had to do was to routinely write appraisal reports with the same procedures.

Naturally a cozy relationship (favorably seen as a relationship of trust) developed between clients and veteran appraisers, and it was almost impossible for other appraisers to try to break such relations and supplant old-timers. Everybody knew that the work from this government office goes to Mr. A, and the requests from that office should go to Mr. B, and so forth.

The national and municipal governments, the client side, also felt comfortable with those particular appraisers and offered optional contracts to them, reasoning that without the particular appraiser the continuity of appraisal work would be affected. As a result, appraisal fees came to be fixed at high levels.

The number of real estate appraisers was increasing year after year, so while clients were closely tied with particular appraisers, newcomers who had come through difficult tests could not find work. They were forced to depend on the veteran appraisers who had trained them and get a tiny share of the boss's work. The boss could maintain their long-time clients by passing on to their henchmen extra work that his office could not handle.

The situation continued until the emergence of new clients and a new system of real estate appraisal reports and appraisal fees. Recently, in the process of privatizing post offices and changing the status of national universities into independent administrative institutions, the government introduced a bidding system for all appraisal work and placed orders accordingly. It was truly epoch-making.

During the past decade, reflecting the trend of getting professional licenses and certificates among many young salaried workers and college students, a large number of people passed the appraiser's test. They don't have to feel restrained by past bonds of appraisal business and act as freely as they feel like. If they feel English is needed for their job, they try to get a certificate in English. If they believe it is beneficial to be a certified public accountant or CPA, they try to pass those tests. They are not confined only in the world of real estate appraisal. Young appraisers of today are broad-minded in doing their business.

Other than those hired by real estate appraisal firms and offices, appraisers who could not make use of their qualifications are now finding new positions as banking institutions and foreign firms have come to actively employ qualified appraisers.

Days have almost come for these young appraisers to replace veteran appraisers.

Appraisers Registered with the Minister and Those Registered with the Governor

Depending on what they actually do, appraisers can be divided into two types: those who are registered with the minister of land and transportation and those who are registered with the governor of a prefecture. Big organizations like banks, real estate companies, and real estate agents that are doing appraisal business as a side business usually register with the minister. Earnings from appraisal fees account for a small percentage of the entire sales of those organizations. They do not intend to live on real estate appraisal fees. Each local branch of those companies has a real estate appraisal department as an outpost, thus forming a network of both sales and real estate appraisal.

These outposts are nothing but ornamental at present and are not doing much selling. However, they do have excellent human resources and accumulated knowledge. If they become independent of their parent companies, they can grab some of the clients of established appraisal companies, and it will affect the industry a great deal.

Of the major firms that are registered with the minister, perhaps Japan Real Estate Institute and Sanyu System will be the only companies that are engaged only in real estate appraisal and its peripheral businesses. Japan Real Estate Institute handled 26,311

Table 10

Appraisal cases handled and amount of sales by top five real estate appraisal companies (registered with the minister)

	Year	Japan Real Estate Institute	Sanyu System	Daiwa Real Estate Appraisal	Tanizawa General Appraisal	Chuo Real Estate Appraisal	Total of those registered wth Minister
No. of cases	2001	5,230	12,258	1,316	1,348	1,263	40,913
	2002	26,392	12,545	4,130	2,688	2,904	78,646
	2003	9,145	11,140	2,325	2,020	1,235	48,953
	2004	10,972	10,117	2,494	2,218	1,143	46,711
	2005	26,311	9,503	5,079	3,306	2,766	75,297
Amount of sales (million yen)	2001	3,364	1,098	694	965	611	13,467
	2002	5,700	1,180	923	1,085	693	17,786
	2003	3,707	956	1,044	1,216	518	14,774
	2004	4,006	979	952	1,371	563	15,098
	2005	4,433	1,091	1,093	1,315	694	17,114
Proceeds per case (thousand yen)	2001	643	90	527	716	484	329
	2002	216	94	223	404	238	226
	2003	405	86	449	602	419	302
	2004	365	97	382	618	492	323
	2005	168	115	215	398	251	227

Number of appraisal firms: 94 in 2001, 93 in 2002, 92 in 2003, 97 in 2004 and 102 in 2005.

(Data from the Ministry of Land, Infrastructure and Transport)

cases in 2005, Sanyu System 9,503 cases and the third-ranked Daiwa Real Estate Appraisal 5,079 cases. (See Table 10 = Surveyed by the National Land and Transportation Ministry.)

Appraisal companies whose offices extend over more than two prefectures and their business activities are nationwide register themselves with the minister. Meanwhile, firms whose activities are local in nature, within a single prefecture, are registered with their governors.

According to the land ministry, as of January 1, 2006, the total number of real estate appraisal companies in Japan was 3,251. Of those, 102 were registered with the minister and the rest were doing business within one prefecture only and registered with their respective governor.

As a result of market expansion for real estate appraisal business, the number of appraisal companies increased from 1,563 in 1980 to 3,251 in 2006.

Companies Registered with Their Governor Have Small Offices

Looking more minutely, the number of those appraisers registered with the minister has increased year by year from 60 to 100 in 1999, after which it started to decline. There are now just a little over ninety firms. The decrease in number of those registered with the ministry after 1999 can be attributed to mergers or bankruptcies of trust banks as well as major real estate companies, or abolition of appraisal departments.

So, most of the increase was by appraisal firms whose business areas were limited and were registered with their governors.

Meanwhile, the number of real estate appraisers who engage in appraisal work is 4,343, and that of assistant real estate appraisers is 771, and their combined total is 5,114. The number of appraisers has increased over the last twenty years by about 2,000, but still, as compared with 15,000 CPAs and 20,000 attorneys, the number of these experts is considerably small.

Of 5,114 appraisers and assistant appraisers, those who are registered with the minister are 1,089 and those registered with their governors number 4,025. This means four-fifths of appraisers belong to appraisal firms registered with the governors.

The average number of appraisers and assistant appraisers per one appraisal business firm is 1.6. The firms registered with the minister employ 11.8 but those registered with governors only 1.3. Whether they are incorporated or not, real estate appraisal offices registered with governors are mostly small in scale with one or two qualified staff.

Remuneration of Real Estate Appraisers

Although the total amount of remuneration of real estate appraisal business increased to 75 billion yen in 2005 for special

Table 11

Remuneration of real estate appraisal firms and the number of cases handled

	Remuneration (billion yen)	# of cases (thousand cases)
1980	16.7	88.0
1985	23.2	117.0
1990	52.1	180.0
1991	54.0	173.0
1992	51.6	161.0
1993	59.9	281.0
1994	49.5	151.0
1995	46.4	144.0
1996	60.1	334.0
1997	43.3	144.0
1998	43.2	151.0
1999	63.6	464.0
2000	44.1	185.0
2001	43.8	191.0
2002	66.2	496.0
2003	46.1	207.0
2004	44.9	203.0
2005	75.0	487.0

Data from the Ministry of Land, Infrastructure and Transport

reasons, one can tell how small an industry it is. (See Table 11 and Graph 2) Breaking it down, those registered with governors earned 57.9 billion yen and those registered with the minister 17.1 billion. Small- and medium-sized appraisal firms account for 77 percent of the income earned by all. When you look at the industry as a whole, the power of those registered with governors is predominant. But the average annual remuneration of all appraisal companies is 14.5 million yen per company, while that for those registered with governors is 10 million yen and that for those registered with the minister is 16 million yen. Major firms registered with the minister are in an advantageous position in terms of the scope of business, processing capabilities, as well as appraisal ability. Consequently they are paid more favorably than smaller

Graph 2
Trend of remuneration received by real estate appraisal firms

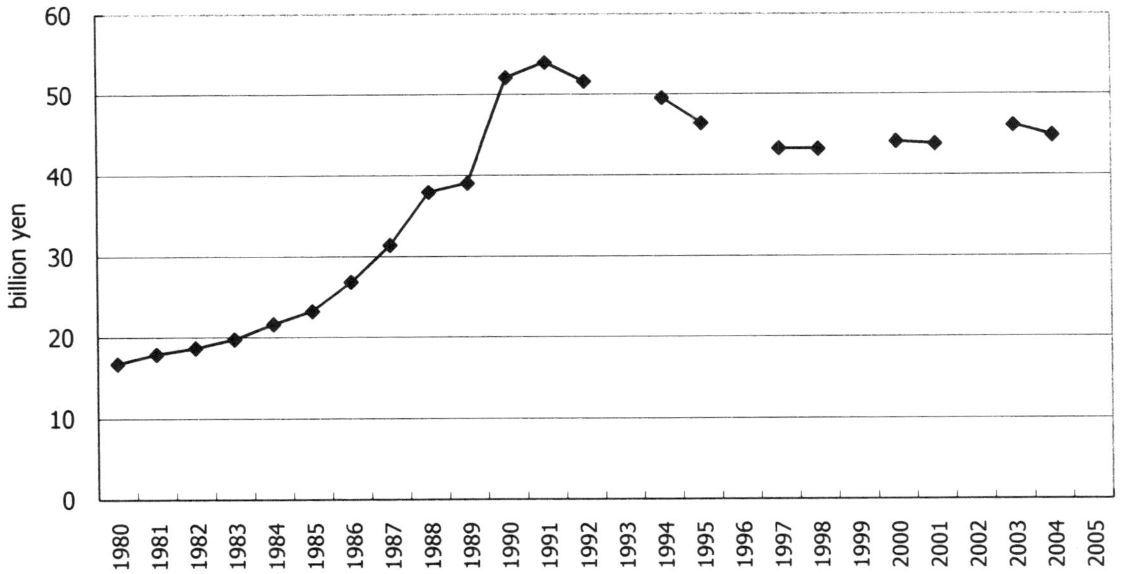

Note: 1993, 1996, 1999, 2002 and 2005 were excluded because continuity of remuneration cannot be secured since they fell on the year when reassessment of fixed property tax was done. (Data from the Ministry of Land, Infrastructure and Transport)

firms. The average remuneration per appraisal case is 141,000 yen for those registered with the governor and 227,000 yen for those registered with the minister. (See Table 11 = By the land ministry.)

The difference in remuneration between major appraisal companies and smaller firms is reflected on the income of each appraiser. The average annual income of appraisers hired by major appraisal firms registered with the minister is 13.6 million yen, while that of appraisers of firms registered with the governor is 7.8 million yen.

In the case of those registered with the minister, each firm gets higher annual revenues. And since each of their appraisal cases is paid more, they can pay better compensation to their appraisers. They can also afford to hire more capable appraisers, which make it possible to handle more difficult appraisal work and their expertise keeps growing. The reverse is the case with smaller appraisal firms registered with their governor.

Suffering from the concentration of appraisal work in major companies, small and medium-sized private appraisal firms have gotten themselves into a fix and now are transforming themselves into subcontractors of major firms.

Dwindling Appraisal Firms Registered with the Governor

Requests for appraisal work from major banking institutions are expected to increase in the future. Since orders are placed by banks' head offices, they will most likely come to major appraisal companies to be processed intensively at their headquarters. Appraisal requests concentrate in major appraisal companies registered with the minister because their main offices are in such mega-cities as Tokyo and Osaka. They are also capable of handling properties in regional cities with their nationwide networks. Even if local appraisal firms registered with the governor visited the branch offices of major banks, there is little hope of getting any business.

The difference in number of appraisal companies between big cities and regional cities is also a problem. The number of those companies in Tokyo totals 874 and Osaka, 328. Putting both together, there are 1,202 companies all together in this category, accounting for 39 percent of the national total. Similarly, the number of appraisers in Tokyo is 1,737 and in Osaka 525. Putting both together, they account for 44 percent of the national total.

On the other hand, in the sparsely populated prefecture of Fukushima, there are only twelve real estate appraisal firms and nineteen appraisers. In Tottori Prefecture, the number of appraisal firms is fourteen and that of appraisers is fifteen. (According to the land ministry, as of January 1, 2004.) The prefecture not having many appraisers are Tottori and Saga with fifteen each, Kochi sixteen, Shimane seventeen, Akita and Fukui nineteen each, Iwate and Yamagata twenty each and Yamanashi twenty-two.

In these prefectures, appraisers are too busy with the requests from public offices and cannot possibly accept requests from the private sectors.

For your information, in Fukushima Prefecture, the remuneration each appraisal firm receives annually is 11 million yen on average and in Tottori 8 million yen. In Tokyo, the average annual compensation of each appraisal firm other than those registered with the minister is 11 million yen and that in Osaka is 9 million yen. So we can say there is not much regional difference in remuneration.

I wonder why those appraisers in Tokyo who do not get much work do not move to regional areas and open their business. In local areas there are not so many appraisers, yet their income is almost the same as the amounts earned by their counterparts in big cities. The living cost is usually much lower in regional cities.

The problem is that it might take them some time to become a member of the local real estate appraisal association if they don't have any territorial connection there. Until they are accepted as a member of the association, they may not be able to accept appraisal requests from public organizations, or they find it difficult to engage in sales activities, or they may not have access to real estate transaction cases or even if they do, they may have to pay expensive fees to see them. Considering all those factors, and the challenge of moving and settling into a new community, it may not be so easy to relocate.

Also, I hear that some local associations ask for a sizable amount of financial contribution as a condition to become their member.

Poorly Paid Government Jobs

I think the readers now have a rough idea of what appraisers are. Then, what about clients?

Clients for real estate appraisal companies can be divided into two groups: public institutions and private sectors.

The payment made to the appraisal industry between January 1, 2003 and December 31 of the same year was 46.1 billion yen. Of this total, the amount that came from public organizations was 18.56 billion (40 percent) and that from private sectors including individuals was 27.54 billion yen.

Of the total amount, 76 percent was received by companies registered with the governor. More minutely, those registered with the governor have received 86 percent of the orders placed by the national government and 83 percent by local public entities. Public organizations must give priority to local businesses and therefore place their orders predominantly with appraisal firms registered with the governor.

Meanwhile, appraisal firms registered with the minister are getting only 45 percent of the orders placed by public corporations

Table 12

Average remuneration per case in 2004 by appraisal orderers

(thousand yen)

	Total	From public organizations	From private sectors
Altogether	154	111	311
Those registered with minister	227	134	376
Those registered with governor	141	108	286

Note: Alhough the up-to-date data available is for 2005, it falls on the year for property tax evaluation which comes every 3 years, therefore the data given here is for 2004.

and government financial corporations, and 28 percent of requests from private sectors including individuals.

The average amount of remuneration paid by public organizations for each appraisal request is 110,000 yen, whereas that by private sectors is 311,000 yen. The work for public institutions is labor intensive. (See Table 12). Also the number of orders private sectors place in a year is 109,061, whereas that by public institutions is 97,820. The reason for low remuneration per item of public properties is because the price per item for adjusting posted and standard land prices is low, but orders from public organizations generally pay much better.

From now on, the number of orders from public organizations are expected to decrease, while banking institutions will give appraisers an increasing number of appraisal work since it will be a general practice for banks to utilize appraisal reports when they offer loans with real estate as collateral. Furthermore, from March 2006, when the going price (market price) of a property owned by a company is lower than its book value, it is to be recorded as a loss. If we consider demand for appraisal work needed for accounting for impaired assets, the weights of order volume from public organizations and private sectors will soon be reversed. As a consequence, sales of appraisal firms could also be reversed between those registered with the governor and those registered with the minister.

Are Thick Appraisal Reports Necessary?

A real estate appraisal report which is the product of an appraisal company and an appraiser is delivered from the appraisal company after real estate appraiser or assistant appraiser indicated his/her qualifications and put his/her signature and seal. In other words, the report has to carry two seals: one for the appraisal company and the other for the appraiser.

An appraisal report called "full-fledged appraisal report" consists of tens of pages and it takes several months to complete as it is written in elaborate language. Since it is thick and looks dignified and scholarly, the appraisal firm can earn as appraisal fees millions of yen or tens of millions of yen for such a report. (See Table 13)

Unlike funds for an undertaking, few housing loan-related cases need such a thick and expensive appraisal report. Real estate appraisal companies had never thought that their appraisal reports would be utilized for housing loans.

The first line of a real estate appraisal report begins with explanatory description of the area where the property is located, and it often includes wordy and irrelevant lines talking about nearby mountains and the sea or giving some historical episodes. For the bankers in charge of housing loans, it is a waste of time to read through it because what they want to know is how much the property is worth on what ground. They also want a report quickly and inexpensively. It is meaningless to mention in a real estate appraisal report whether the property in question commands the view of Mt. Fuji.

Table 13
Rapid calculation table of basic appraisal fees under the regulation for real estate appraisal fees

Type	Buildings & Lots		Sectional Ownership Bldg.	
	Rate	Additional amount	Rate	Additional Amount
Below 5 million yen	—	176 thou yen	—	176 thou yen
Above 5 million, below 10million yen	88/10 thou	132 thou yen	88/10 thou	132 thou yen
Above 10 million, below 20 million yen	44/10 thou	176 thou yen	88/10 thou	132 thou yen
Above 20 million, below 40 million yen	44/10 thou	176 thou yen	88/10 thou	220 thou yen
Above 40 million, below 80 million yen	22/10 thou	264 thou yen	88/10 thou	308 thou yen
Above 80 million, below 150 million yen	12.6/10 thou	340 thou yen	88/10 thou	384 thou yen
Above 150 million, below 300 million yen	5.8/10 thou	442 thou yen	88/10 thou	486 thou yen
Above 300 million, below 600 million yen	5.7/10 thou	445 thou yen	88/10 thou	489 thou yen
Above 600 million, below 1.2 billion yen	3/10 thou	607 thou yen	88/10 thou	651 thou yen
Above 1.2 bilion, below 2.5 billion yen	1.9/10 thou	739 thou yen	88/10 thou	783 thou yen
Above 2.5 billion yen	1.4/10 thou	864 thou yen	88/10 thou	883 thou yen

Simplified Appraisal Report

According to real estate appraisal standards, the number of items that are really needed for a real estate appraisal report is limited. From the very beginning of the company, we at Sanyu System worked out necessary items and their guidelines for appraisal reports so that one can only fill in necessary information. Eliminating unnecessary lines as much as we could, we devised several unified appraisal patterns for single-family homes as well as for condominiums.

As a result, we were able to reduce the number of pages from tens to several pages, which in turn saved appraisers' time and labor. Naturally, appraisal fees could be lowered.

It was about that time that Japan Real Estate Appraisal Association also completed its own simplified appraisal form on a commercial basis. (May 1980)

The items to be provided in the simplified appraisal report forms of both the real estate appraisal association and Sanyu System were almost identical. But Sanyu System, as we focused our business on banking institutions, tried to differentiate our appraisal report form by providing as an attachment a survey form for such information as settlement of mortgage and list of joint mortgage entered in Section B (matters on various rights are entered) of a certified copy of register.

The simplified appraisal forms prepared by the real estate appraisal association were available to all members of the association, but those who actually made use of them were not many, because the association itself did not accept appraisal requests. Forms were made but they were hardly used. In the meantime, Sanyu System received a large number of orders for appraisal work and assigned some of the work to part-time appraisers. They used appraisal report forms that we had made.

We will explain who these part-time appraisers are in chapter 7. They are not employees of Sanyu, but are on contract to Sanyu for individual cases of work and have registered with our network. Even though real estate appraisers and assistant appraisers wanted to do appraisal work for banking institutions, not many visited them to get orders for appraisal work and not many made use of appraisal report forms at the association.

Generally speaking, real estate appraisers are not good at sales pitches even if they know that banks are in need of real estate appraisal reports to meet increasing demand for private housing loans. Particularly, many of those who became appraisers during the Showa era (approximately before 1990s) find it difficult to be sociable and chose the profession as it doesn't require talking with people as much.They hate sales work but they love writing appraisal reports quietly.

Those who joined us as part-time appraisers have left to Sanyu their selling job. It was like the separation of production (making appraisal reports) and sales (seeking orders for appraisal work). It was for this reason that Sanyu has been able to enjoy a leading position in the business with banking institutions for more than ten years.

After around 1980s when financial institutions began to make much use of real estate appraisal, real estate appraisal business grew out of a mere business of writing bureaucratic documents to be submitted to the government office, and established itself as a much needed business in the economic system. The modernization of real estate appraisal business has thus begun.

6
Auction Market

Unpopular Auction Items

The real estate market is made up of buyers and sellers. Between the buyers and sellers are the real estate agents. Those three parties constitute the market. Both buyers and sellers can freely use this market.

Markets with buyers and sellers are typical in a capitalistic society. Price trends are set in this market through the aggregation of individual prices, which are, in turn, set through exchanges between buyers and sellers. There is, however, a strange aspect to Japan's property market that is not ruled only by these principles of supply and demand. That is the auction market as applied to properties whose owners face financial difficulty. When debtors become insolvent, creditors—which in Japan are mainly banking institutions—petition a court to foreclose on the mortgage and the property backing the mortgage is auctioned to new buyers.

Even if there are few or no buyers, an auction must take place if there is something to be sold. Those who sell under Japan's auction system are not the owners, but the banks who own the loans backing properties held by an owner in default. The court acts as a broker. Beyond the debtors, creditors, and the court, the other main participants in this market are the bidders.

When an insolvent debtor must sell a mortgaged property to pay off debts, the debtor will try to do so before banking institutions file a petition with the court for an auction. This is largely so that the debtor can avoid disclosing the sort of intimate and embarrassing details that must be disclosed in a court auction of a mortgaged property.

They also know they will suffer a loss if the property is sold by auction since prices at auction are normally considerably lower than those at non-auction real estate market. Sometimes, a debtor or owner will seek to sell a property that might have been passed down through generations to a relative rather than sell it off in the open market.

Banking institutions have experienced a number of downturns in the property market in postwar years, some big and some small in scale. But they often avoid seeking to recover bad loans by selling the property linked to the loan through the auction system, because doing so might offend a debtor. Besides, it also carries reputation risk for the bank, by appearing to be too tough in extracting money from the debtor.

The auction system often takes more time than the alternative, and can cost court fees and attorney payments, which are often considerable. The laws and rules in Japan don't allow for the easy removal of occupants of rental properties, so forcibly evicting through the court system isn't a reliably quick way of recovering funds. A creditor often has little idea of how long it might take to evict a tenant. Sometimes the court sets the minimum bid at 60 percent or 70 percent of the comparable prices on the market. So rather than use the courts, banking institutions tend to encourage troubled borrowers to sell property voluntarily.

During the bubble, if a financial institution was forced to resort to auction to solve a bad loan, it would have been branded as a poorly run institution incapable of measuring the borrower's ability to repay the debt at the time the loan was extended. A bank forced to sell a property at auction was considered such a failure that the president was often forced to resign his position.

Needless to say, if the value of a property goes up on a regular real estate market and exceeds the price at which it was bought or the amount of money that the debtor owes to the bank, the borrower would merely sell the property on the market and pay the debt to the bank. The bank would have little need for the auction system.

Thus, there were few cases of auctions while real estate prices were on the rise. During those days, properties that were up for auction had more to do with forces other than the strict economic rules of the market, perhaps a corporate contest with a rival, or in-fighting between family members.

In postwar years until the growing period of the bubble, the auction market was thus little used, didn't grow, and grabbed little attention in the property market. It just functioned quietly.

Auction Items are Popular Among the People of Osaka

The number of bidders was rather small, too, because of a number of reasons. First, the property could have troubled with organized criminals or other shady tenants. Second, auctioned items were often considered sub-par properties. Third, most customers preferred to buy properties on the open market rather than deal with the costs of the courts. Fourth, many didn't understand the procedures of the court, and thus tended to avoid it. Fifth, the system provides no system for a prospective buyer to confirm the content or real condition of the property and thus buyers might be uncertain what they might be bidding for. And sixth, the court allows little time between the notification of its intent to hold an auction and the actual auction, allowing for little prospect of conducting due diligence.

The system, however, caused many misunderstandings. A real property involved in a troubled transaction is different from a car involved in an accident. A car involved in an accident breaks. However, the trouble of a real property was caused by the fact that the owner—the borrower—didn't pay back the money owed to the creditor, and therefore the property itself is usually not defective. But in Japan, a property can be considered sub-standard simply because it was being sold at auction.

There is an interesting phenomenon observed among bidders in Tokyo and Osaka that underscores this prejudice.

When we look at the ratio of successful bids by corporations and those by private individuals in Tokyo and Osaka, the success rate among individual bidders in Tokyo stood at 30.9 percent in the first half of 1998 when the percentage of successful individual bidders was at its peak, whereas in Osaka 44.6 percent. Osaka's peak came in the latter half of 2001 and that year Osaka's percentage was 46.5 percent and Tokyo, 22.6 percent. Individual successful bidders in Osaka were 14 percent to 24 percent more than those of Tokyo (Surveyed by Sanyu System Real Estate Finance Institute).

This was because Tokyo bidders don't like to be associated with having bought a property at cheaper prices than normal through an auction. Instead of registering in their individual names, they have their agents purchase property once and buy that from the agents even if it is a little more expensive.

On the other hand, it seems that bidders in Osaka try to buy property as cheaply as possible and brag about it.

Grudge of Financial Institutions

At present, most of the clients of Sanyu are financial institutions and more than half of the requests for property appraisal have to do with bad loans. The properties are mostly bad loan collateral that banks don't even want to see. Even if they were able to sell them, the maximum they can recover would be somewhere between 10 percent or 20 percent. The banks have to ask appraisal companies to evaluate such properties and pay appraisal fees.

We hate to be blamed for any problems we didn't create, but from the bank's perspective, having to pay an appraisal fee makes them feel they are throwing good money after bad. And while we are not creditors at Sanyu, I can understand their stress and anger. It is true that they should have checked out their borrowers more thoroughly, but those who were in charge of extending the loan are often transferred and long gone by the time the loan goes bad. Their successors can't be blamed. Yet, we can't do the appraisal for nothing. We often feel that we are being unfairly singled out for criticism.

The Financial Services Agency, prosecutors, and police are more severe these days and unless they process cases based on prices appraised by a third party, the responsible people at the bank might be accused of a breach of trust. So banks increasingly treat appraisal fees as business expenses. Particularly for such smaller financial institutions as cooperative banks and credit associations, it seems more beneficial to outsource the job of appraisal rather than hiring their own appraisers.

Auction Market after the Bubble Burst

When a price decline lasts as long, and spreads as widely and extensively, as the recent slide in Japan's property values, the auction system has a sudden flood of properties that need to be sold off.

Studying the reasons that properties have been filed for auction, we found, in addition to cases in which debtors became insolvent, not a small number of emotional troubles caused by the fact that at the time of financing, banks acted as intermediaries and made debtors buy expensive properties. So bankers and borrowers pointed fingers at each other. One big reason for this: banks played the role of real estate agent.

After the bubble, insolvent debtors must have tried hard to

sell their properties, but as prices continued to slide, they must have felt it difficult to accept how far and fast the value of their holding had fallen, and what it might mean for their own livelihood.

Meanwhile, banking institutions could not take a high-handed attitude at first, thinking of the circumstances at the time of financing as well as their long standing business relations. Yet, when bad loans piled up so badly as to threaten their solvency, they had little choice but to dispose of them through auction. In order to dispose of a large number of bad loans, the auction system was attractive because it required no negotiation with debtors.

Viewing things calmly, I must say that banks that took a hard-line approach at an earlier stage were able to survive, but those that took a lenient posture either went bankrupt or were absorbed by other organizations.

As all banking institutions actively made use of auctions, their psychological resistance to the auction system dissipated. Also, when selling a property voluntarily, the agreement by all parties concerned is necessary, including the owner of the property, all secured parties, renters, and occupants. It takes time for everyone to reach a consensus, whereas auction has no such requirement and can be processed automatically and speedily. Banks became familiar with procedures involved in auction and, by eventually cutting out lawyers from the process, realized considerable expense savings. They also learned that voluntary selling of properties cost more money than expenses involved in filing for auction. For example, the cost of evictions and voiding mortgages can really add up.

The lowest selling prices determined by the court are 30 percent to 40 percent lower than market prices, but the prices of successful bidding are 30 percent higher than the court prices (according to a survey by Sanyu System Real Estate Finance Institute). So, the final bidding prices are usually 10 percent to 20 per-

Table 14
Change in the number of bid openings at Tokyo and Osaka District Courts

(cases)

	Tokyo	Osaka
1994	3,933	NA
1995	7,137	NA
1996	9,479	4,489
1997	11,049	4,578
1998	12,232	5,180
1999	11,082	5,952
2000	8,734	4,388
2001	6,385	4,138
2002	6,338	4,084
2003	5,783	3,791
2004	4,315	3,582
2005	NA	3,185
***2006**	1,806	1,526

* The figures for 2006 are for first half only.

cent lower than market prices and thus the recovered amounts weren't so small anymore. Furthermore, laws restricting a tenant's rights were strengthened and modified, contributing to the improvement of recovery rate through auction.

Although applications for auction were few and the courts held only a limited number of bids during the Showa era (before 1990), after the burst of the bubble the number of bid openings increased year after year (see Table 14—surveyed by Sanyu System Real Estate Finance Institute).

The number of annual bid openings by Tokyo District Court was, at its peak in 1998, more than 12,000 (total mortgage value was 7 trillion 130 billion yen) and that by Osaka District Court, whose peak was 5,900 one year after Tokyo in 1999.

At the peak, the period of time auction property was held at the court (from the time the court accepted application for auction until the opening of its bid) was twenty-three months for the first half of 1999 at Tokyo District Court and seventeen months for the first half of 2000 at Osaka District Court, according to a survey by Sanyu System Real Estate Finance Institute.

The time a property is held up at Tokyo District Court is approximately 1.5 times longer than at Osaka. This means that when filing for auction with Tokyo District Court, you cannot recover your bad loans as fast as you can at Osaka District Court.

Thus, while the regular market was suffering from a slump, a very special market where sellers came first and buyers came later grew fast to become an enormous and unusual auction market.

Lowest Selling Price and Successful Bidding Price

In Japan, the real estate market and the rice market are the only markets in which there are two different prices for the same article and in one of which the national government is involved in determining prices. The fact that two markets exist for the same commodity is hampering the sound formation of real estate prices.

There are two kinds of auction prices. One is the lowest price for selling and the other is the price of successful bidding.

The lowest price for selling determined by the court indicates to bidders the lowest price they can bid for the property in question. The reason for providing the lowest price for selling is to protect the owner or debtor, who is considered to be in a weak position. The lowest selling price is determined by the evaluator designated by the court.

Most evaluators are real estate appraisers, but some are veteran court clerks appointed by the court. Evaluators form a kind of cartel at each district court and do not welcome an increase in the number of evaluators, which is often said to be a principal cause of prolonged trials.

When the price of an item at auction is not allowed to fall to the level of the bids because of the minimum price stipulation, the transaction is carried over to the next session. The lowest price for selling at the next session can be decided, for example, by lowering a certain percentage from the previous price or having the price reduction set by the evaluators. The specific method is left to each district court to set for itself.

The method of determining the level of the lowest selling price can vary depending on venues of those concerned, but the price of each court is more or less the same discount to the market price.

Court Circumstances

If too many auction items are left unsold and held up there, the court can be criticized for inefficiency and will have to open bids a number of times causing an increase in clerical work. So their true intention is to have properties knocked down to bidders with as few auction sales as possible. At the same time, they have to show an attitude of protecting the weak. What they have in mind for the lowest bidding price seems to be around 60 percent to 70 percent of the market price.

Normally, real estate agents try to close a transaction at as high a price as possible so that their commission will also be high, but the court that is supposed to be a go-between for auction properties wants to sell them quickly even at low prices so as to keep held-up properties at a low level.

As for the fact that there are not many bidders, several reasons can be considered. One reason is, of course, that auction items are considered to be troubled properties, and thus discourage many customers. Other than this, the auction system itself has problems.

First, the time given between the announcement of bidding and the close of bidding (four to five weeks at Tokyo District Court) is too short to allow a sufficient study of the property; second, since the buyer isn't allowed to enter the buildings to be auctioned, physical confirmation of the property's quality is impossible; third, an insufficient examination of the property makes it difficult to determine an appropriate price; fourth, when bidders wants to consult a real estate agent for advice, they become anxious about consultation fees since there is no standard for such payments unlike commissions for real estate transactions; fifth, there are few set rules for payments to agents in case the bidding was not successful; sixth, after successfully closing the bid, time given for its payment is short (within a month at Tokyo District Court), and some bidders find it difficult to come up with the money for it on such short notice; and seventh, the choice of properties is limited as compared with normal markets, etc.

Those who want to take part in bidding have to be aware of the greater risks involved over regular markets because of the many hurdles facing them such as not knowing available quantity, not being able to confirm the quality, limited time, the need to raise funding quickly, and so forth.

Recently some have called for the system of setting the lowest selling price to be abandoned. Some say it should be made possible for anyone to enter an auction even with one yen, while others propose that "the lowest selling price" be changed to "the standard price for selling" and if a bidding price is higher than 80 percent of the standard price, the bidding can be closed. It is very likely that a system other than the lowest selling price system currently used will be instituted in the near future.

If the lowest bidding price is abolished, real estate appraisers will be the hardest hit, but it will benefit financial institutions carrying many bad debts because they can process them faster. Debtors (collateral providers), however, will suffer because the prices of their collateral properties will be slashed.

Movement of Successful Bidding Prices

The price at which bidding is closed at auction is the highest of all bids and is naturally higher than the lowest selling price.

The ratio of the highest bid against the lowest selling price at

Table 15

Multiplying ratio of successful bidding price to lowest selling price at Tokyo District Court

(times)

	Ratio
1994	1.39
1995	1.29
1996	1.34
1997	1.31
1998	1.20
1999	1.25
2000	1.27
2001	1.33
2002	1.37
2003	1.36
2004	1.62
2005	NA
***2006**	1.83

* 2006 is fast half only.

Tokyo District Court (highest bid/lowest selling price) was 1.39 times in 1994 and in 1998 it went down to 1.20. In 1999, it started to turn the other way around and in 2004, 1.62 times and in 2006, 1.83 times, surpassing the level of 1994 (see Table 15—surveyed by Sanyu System Real Estate Finance Institute).

Even setting the lowest selling price at 60 percent of the market price during the bubble, the highest bid will be around 80 percent of the market price. If the lowest selling price is set at 70 percent of the market price, the bid would be closed at 90 percent of the market price. (Surveyed by Sanyu System Real Estate Finance Institute.)

Successful bidding prices at an auction market are 20 percent to 30 percent higher than the impression we get from the lowest selling price.

The Lowest Selling Price That Disturbs the Real Estate Market

Both the lowest selling price and the price of a successful bid are made public, but what attracts people's attention is the lowest selling price, which is announced before the highest bid. Strangely, not many people pay much attention to the price at which a property was actually sold.

Here is an interesting phenomenon. Supposing that Room A of a certain condominium was put on sale at 50 million yen. The price is quite normal and everyone thinks it will be sold within a year. Now Room B, which is next to Room A, has come up for auction. Several people came to the caretaker for information. Everybody in the condominium knows the lowest bidding price is 30 million yen. Putting aside how much Room B was sold for at the end, at least Room A wouldn't have been sold for more than 30 million yen.

When Room C is put on sale, it will be about the same price as Room A. The lowest selling price at one place affects the price level of the same area. However, after being transacted at 30 million yen, the same property might be sold for 40 million yen at auction.

The question of how much more the highest bid is from the lowest selling price and what price level it is against the going price is a big problem, which can disturb normal real estate prices and can deal a big blow to the recovery of bad loans by banking institutions.

In view of an increase in the number of bid openings at the auction market, the government should try to shrink the market itself.

Our experience tells us that the auction market should be improved in several areas. For example, when a debtor is notified of the decision to hold a compulsory auction, the debtor receives several letters from real estate agents recommending that the debtor should sell the property voluntarily, despite the fact that the information regarding auction has not been made public. When this sort of thing happens, how can a sound market be promoted? An information leak like this is, in fact, quite possibly illegal. Something must be done to remedy such a situation and efforts should be made to shrink the auction market.

Impression of Successful Bidders

A property that isn't sold successfully because a bid failed to come in above the minimum is held over to the next court session, which can take weeks, or even months.

Sanyu System Real Estate Finance Institute carried out three questionnaire surveys of private individuals who were successful bidders at auction held by Tokyo District Court. Tables 16 and 17 show some interesting points from the survey in November 2001, the most recent of the three.

The number of successful bids is on the decrease after hitting a peak in 1998 in Tokyo and in 1999 in Osaka. After the bubble burst, changes of the auction market were indicated not only in the number of bid openings but in bid winning ratio (number of winning bids/number of bid openings). (Table 18—surveyed by Sanyu System Real Estate Finance Institute.)

Over time, what is characteristic of the change in winning ratio are: 1) it hit the bottom in 1998 and turned upward thereafter, 2) the ratio for every winning bid in Osaka seems to be higher than Tokyo, 3) Tokyo's ratio was catching up with the level of Osaka, and 4) during the first half of 2002, the winning ratio of both district courts exceeded 60 percent.

Of all the properties up for auction now, half of them should be successful in meeting bids for each offering.

The rise and fall of the winning ratio, and the period that sales

Table 16

Successful individual bidders of real properties located in Metropolitan Tokyo from October 2000 to July 2001.

(Out of 849 asked, 96 replied. Collection was 11%)

▸ Ages of successful bidders:

50s – 36% 60s – 33% 40s – 20%

▸ Professions of successful bidders:

Self-employed – 36% Private company – 34% Inoccupation – 11%

▸ Annual income of successful bidders:

Below 10 million yen – 45% Less than 5 million yen – 26% 10 million ~ below 20 million yen – 14%

▸ Motives for taking part in auction:

"From TV programs, Newspaper articles and conversation with friends and acquaintances" – about 50%

Explanation: Majority were influenced by the mass media. Few were recommended by real estate agents, lawyers and accountants.

▸ Reason for taking part in auction:

"Relatively cheap" – 56% "Close to home" – 16%

Explanation: Less than 10% had vested interest in properties. The fact that those who answered "Relatively cheap" were quite a few had been anticipated. "Close to home" was because they can check out the property easily. Also, management after acquisition is easy.

▸ Persons to consult with:

"No one" – 27% "Real estate agents" – 27%

Explanation: Those who do not consult at all are either professionals or semi-professionals.

▸ Professions of those who did not consult with anyone:

Private firms – 36% Self-employed – 21%

Explanation: Private firms probably means running an apartment and self-employed, real estate Agents.

▸ Properties for which they did not consult with anyone:

"Condominiums"- 60% The rest are either "one-unit homes" and "commercial properties."

▸ Properties successfully contracted:

"Condominiums"- 55% "One-unit homes"- 19%

Explanation: Condominiums and one-unit homes are easy items for auction as they are readily usable.

▸ Successful bidding prices:

Below 10 million yen – 43% 10 to 20 million yen – 14% Above 100 million yen – 8%

Explanation: Most of those that are below 10 million yen are condominiums. Some but not many are one-unit homes. Those above 100 million yen are commercial properties. Main purchasers are those earning less than 10 million yen and their bidding is for properties less than 10 million yen.

▸ The number of successful biddings in the past:

"One"- 33%　　"4 or more"- 26%

Explanation: Those who answered "4 or more" are supposedly professionals.

▸ The number of biddings before they succeeded:

First time – 56%　　Second time – 22%

Explanation: First try and successful were 56% and including 2nd try nearly 80% were successful.

▸ Is auction your business?:

"No"- 91%

Explanation: Many successful bidders appeared to be professional, but they deny it.

▸ How would the property be used?:

"Investment (Renting out)" – 49%　　"Personal use" – 31%　　"Investment(Reselling)" – 13%

Explanation: 60% of "Investment(Renting out)" are condominiums. Nearly 70% of those who answered "Investment(Renting out)" were over 50 years old. Commercial properties account for 20%. Not many people seem to think of buying a property at a low price and selling it high

▸ How did you raise funds.:

"own fund" – 56%　　"Partial loan" – 34%　　"All loan" – 10%

Explanation: They either have enough money or bidding prices were low. Majority managed to pay from their own funds.

▸ Where did you borrow from?:

"Banks" – 37%　　"Credit cooperatives or credit associations" – 27%　　"Friends, acquaintances, relatives" – 22%

Explanation: They do not seem to have difficulty in borrowing.

▸ Collateral for borrowing?:

"Property obtained by bidding" –65%　　"Other properties" – 28%　　"Property obtained by another successful bid" – 7%

Explanation: The fact that they use other real properties than successfully bid properties for collateral means that they own other properties.

▸ Will you use it if public funds are available?:

"Will use" – 58%　　"Will not use" – 42%

Explanation: Even if public funds should become available in the future, more than 40% of people do not seem to be interested in utilizing them. Whatever factors that discourage them from using the funds must be remedied.

▸ Having take part in auction, what is your impression?:

"Was difficult." – 31%　　"Just as I expected." – 30%　　"Easier than expected." – 30%

Explanation: Examining such comments as "Difficult" and "Just as I expected (prepared myself)," the court should take appropriate measures for improvement.

▸ What did you think was difficult?:

"Deciding bidding prices" – 29%　　"Eviction after bidding was over" –16%

"Confirmation of occupants" – 14%

Explanation: These are concrete examples of the above comments. There were a dozen Different comments. Will be talked more about this later.

▸ What did you think of successful bidding prices?:

"Appropriate" – 47%   "Too high" – 32%   "Very reasonable" –· 21%

Explanation: Although 50% were satisfied with their price, there were also more people who regretted having bid too high than people who are happy about their purchase.

▸ How long did it take from the bid closing until actual acquisition of the property?:

"2 months" – 45%   "1 month, 3 months" – 14% each

Explanation: A few months are needed before you get a property. Procedures within the court should be improved.

▸ Any defects or damages with the property?:

"None" – 43%   "Yes (If seen before bidding, could have told.)" – 44%

"Yes (Even seen before, could not have told.)" – 13%

Explanation: 40% of those problems could have been solved, if previous checking had been possible. This is an institutional problem. People concerned should try their ingenuity at solving it.

▸ What kind of defects?:

"Dilapidated inside" – 55%   "Unlawful occupants" – 23%   "Others" – 22%

Explanation: As for dilapidation, photos should be available on the court's checking report on physical condition The question is whether somebody depredated it after the checking or the examiner did not show a real picture. It could be the court's poor control.

▸ Were there occupants?

"Yes (Knew in advance)" – 62%   Yes (Learned after bidding was closed)" – 10%   "No" – 28%

Explanation: Many had previous knowledge about occupants

▸ Do you want occupants to be removed?:

"Yes and no" – 70%   "Welcome" – 30%

Explanation: For condominium investors, occupants could be renters and are supposed to be welcome 70% of them ,however, are at a loss.

▸ How is the situation on evacuation?:

"Took time to have them move out" – 39%   "Still occupying" – 37%   "Moved out quickly" – 24%

Explanation: Three quarters of people needed time to have occupants move out. Laws have been Improved lately and if this problem is solved, auction will be carried on smoothly.

▸ What would be your requests to the government or the court?:

"Wish we could check property in advance." – 13%   "Legislation for eviction." – 10%

"Clearly identify occupants." – 8%   17 other requests

Explanation: Shouldn't the court be concerned only with matters that require state power such as "transfer of ownership" and "cancellation of mortgage," leaving other matters to private hands such as receiving requests for auction, determining lowest bidding prices, office work relating to publication of information, and bidding procedures in general.

Table 17
Problems felt after successful bidding.

Problems felt.	
No preview was possible.	22.7%
Delinquent service charge to be borne.(Condominium)	22.1%
Having occupant evacuate and paying expenses for it.	19.6%
Slow court procedure.	10.4%
None	8.0%
Returning shop guarantee money.	4.9%
Difference between dossier and assertion of occupant.	4.3%
Necessity of on-the-spot survey.	1.8%
Annoyance felt against competing brokers and real estate	1.8%
After bidding was closed, it was found out that the property was for statutory surface right.	0.6%
Others	3.7%
Total	**100.0%**

are held up at the courts, all influence creditors, debtors, and the nation's economy.

Suppose the normal land price declines by 5 percent in six months after the bursting of the bubble. If unsuccessful bidders have to wait another six months until the next opening of bids or the property held up at the court needs additional six months for the opening of next bids, the lowest selling price will drop by another 5 percent while everybody waits for the court system to open a new round of bidding, and thus the recovery price also falls by 5 percent.

As time goes by, a recovery amount declines by 5 percent from what it should be and both the creditor and debtor lose 5 percent despite every intention of selling off the property that is bogged down in the court system.

From the viewpoint of the national economy, the decline of bid winning rates and the prolonged time over which properties are held up at court, are causing economic losses measured in the

Table 18
Change in ratio of closed bids

		Tokyo	Osaka
1996	1st half	46.0%	50.6%
	2nd half	49.8%	51.1%
1997	1st half	51.1%	51.6%
	2nd half	48.8%	46.1%
1998	1st half	42.6%	44.3%
	2nd half	45.9%	42.1%
1999	1st half	51.2%	49.1%
	2nd half	52.3%	52.9%
2000	1st half	57.3%	56.7%
	2nd half	56.1%	56.9%
2001	1st half	60.2%	56.9%
	2nd half	57.7%	59.6%
2002	1st half	62.2%	63.7%
	2nd half	61.3%	65.1%
2003	1st half	62.4%	62.4%
	2nd half	64.3%	67.1%
2004	1st half	66.3%	66.2%
	2nd half	68.1%	71.1%
2005	1st half	NA	71.0%
	2nd half	77.3%	73.8%
2006	1st half	78.6%	80.2%

trillions of yen. Knowing these facts, efforts to analyze the auction system for minimizing such losses seems to be very important even for working out strategy for national economy.

I first thought the fact that the ratio of successful bidding was rising every year was due to an increase in the number of bidders, but it wasn't quite so. We checked how many bidders were in-

Table 19

Number of auctions by number of bidders at Osaka District

No. of bidders	No of auctions		
	2nd half 1998	1st half 2002	1st half 2006
1	469	307	66
2	225	170	67
3	122	139	71
4	93	94	67
5	75	83	86
6	45	69	63
7	27	43	80
8	30	38	63
9	17	32	52
10	16	35	51
Sub total	**1,119**	**1,010**	**666**
Percentage	**92.6%**	**81.1%**	**59.7%**
11	24	28	51
12	5	22	39
13	11	28	39
14	2	25	46
15	5	18	30
16	4	16	31
17	8	13	23
18	6	14	28
19	6	10	22
20	3	4	21
Sub total	**74**	**178**	**330**
Percentage	**6.1%**	**14.3%**	**29.6%**
21	3	11	12
22	3	3	15
23	2	3	14
24	0	6	16
25	2	7	9
26	0	4	9
27	1	1	2
28	1	5	5
29	0	2	8
30	0	3	7
Sub total	**12**	**45**	**97**
Percentage	**1.0%**	**3.6%**	**8.7%**
30 <	2	6	23
40 <	1	6	0
Total	**1,208**	**1,245**	**1,116**
Largest number of bidders	45	89	39
No. of bidders per auction	4	6	10

volved in one successful bidding.

Since information from Tokyo District Court was not available, let us compare the numbers of bidders per successful bidding at Osaka District Court in the second half of 1998 with those in the first half of 2006. (See Table 19—surveyed by Sanyu System Real Estate Finance Institute.)

In the second half of 1998, when the ratio of successful bidding was the lowest in recent years, the number of bidders per successful bid was 3.71. In the first half of 2006, it was 10.3. The number of bidders has increased considerably. The reason for an increase in the ratio of successful tenders could be that people turned to auction items because thcy were finding it rather difficult to obtain properties they liked on the regular market. A high ratio of successful tenders is good for banking institutions because it means faster recovery of bad loans. It is good for the court too since there will be less auction items to stay there.

One other important factor, though not explained in detail, is that depending on the ups and downs of real estate prices, there can be two seasons for auction market: when there are few properties to be auctioned and when there are too many to be handled. If judges, court clerks, evaluators, and enforcers are allocated to match a slack season, they will not be able to handle everything when the number of auction items increases, inviting dissatisfaction from creditors. Conversely, if the court is staffed to match a busy season, when the slack season comes, they will be criticized at parliament or by the mass media for wasting personnel expenditure.

This seasonal difference also affects private real estate agents. Even if they wanted to specialize in real property for auction, they can never be sure whether they will be busy or verging on bankruptcy during a slack season. The auction market is something you cannot control with your sales effort, which is a reason that the number of real estate agents who specialize in auction property never grows.

7

An Appropriate Attitude of Real Estate Appraisal Business

Part-Time Real Estate Appraisers

In 1980, I left Misawa Home after working there for nearly seven years and, at the age of forty-two, founded a real estate appraisal company named Sanyu Systems Housing Loan. At that time, my goal was to create a business of housing finance. To succeed, I believed real estate appraisal would be essential. So I started a real estate appraisal business.

After solidifying the foundation of the company with a business of real estate appraisal and surveys, the next step was to invest the proceeds in the field of housing loan guarantees. If we could still make money, we would finally get into the business of financing housing so that we would have a company with three pillars: appraisals, guarantees, and house financing.

When we established the company, there was a boom in such housing items as subdivisions, houses for sale, and condominiums and the number of housing loans was on the increase. However, as mentioned in chapter 5, real estate appraisal reports issued by appraisers were out of date. Appraisal work took time and the fees were quite high. So, just to appraise a collateral property for a small housing loan, banks were not in a position to utilize expensive appraisal reports.

Meanwhile, as a newcomer, Sanyu System had connections

with neither the central government nor local municipalities and other government organs, and so we found it difficult to increase clients through public organizations. I had thought housing loans would be a promising product in the future, so we focused our attention to banking institutions as our clients.

Since I had worked for Nihon Seimei Life Insurance and engaged in financing business before I entered Misawa Home, I could carry on a conversation smoothly with people from financial institutions. I could talk on the same footing with them and I could understand their sentiments.

I tried to think as if I were a client from a banking institution; what would I want for a real estate appraisal product? I narrowed down my thoughts to the following five points:

1. It must be accurate.
2. An appraisal fee must be within the range of a housing loan commission (30 to 50 thousand yen per case in those days).
3. Since we must compete with other banks, response must be fast.
4. All areas and all properties in the country should be covered.
5. Products (contents, fees) should be diversified so that clients will have a wider choice.

In order to produce appraisal and survey reports to meet those requirements, our conclusion was not to keep full-time appraisers attached to our firm but to organize appraisers throughout Japan as a great team of part-time or entrusted appraisers. This system is based on the idea I got from the founder of Misawa Home, Mr. Chiyoharu Misawa.

Misawa Home tried as much as possible not to invest in its local sales companies, but rather to have locally established firms set up as affiliates. That way, Misawa could minimize their fund requirements and at the same time take advantage of established names in selling their products. The idea was to kill two birds with one stone.

The part-time appraisal of Sanyu was basically a variation on the same idea. By adopting part-time systems, all kinds of merits were enjoyed.

1. Local appraisers were fully aware of the area in question and therefore accurate appraisal was possible.
2. Since the job was to be done locally, no business trips were necessary and accordingly no transportation expenses and no per diem. So the appraisal fees could be smaller, making it possible to set the fee charged to banking institutions at a low level.
3. Living in the area where a property is located, the part-time appraiser could do the job quickly.
4. If part-time appraisers are stationed throughout the country, any appraisal requests could be handled.
5. For Sanyu System personnel expenses do not have to be wasted even during the slack season.

These were the benefits. On the other hand, part-time appraisers themselves would also benefit from this system.

1. Even those who are not confident about sales work can have their office as an independent appraiser.
2. They don't have to work at low pay under tutorial appraisers.
3. As long as they do the work and submit a report, they are paid on 25th of the following month by Sanyu System.
4. What they receive from Sanyu can be treated as a salary and the earnings through their own sales as a special bonus.

5. Sales work would all be handled by Sanyu, so they can concentrate on appraisal work.
6. Since they are not employees of Sanyu, they can turn down our requests if they are busy with other work.

We had our affiliated appraisers concentrate on making good reports. As mentioned before, many appraisers like to make appraisal reports by themselves. Even if they know there is demand for appraisal work at financial institutions, they are not good at making sales calls themselves. That is why we have them buckle down to making appraisal reports which they are good at.

Sales work, checking the contents, billing client banks, payment to appraisers, etc. were all done by Sanyu.

What is most important for Sanyu System is to standardize appraisal methods for our affiliate appraisers and to equalize all appraisal fees. All our efforts were directed to this matter. Through this division of labor, so to speak, affiliate part-time appraisers could minimize their monetary concerns and fees for appraisal reports could be kept to low levels. In addition, Sanyu System was able to earn a reasonable profit.

As had been expected, this outsourcing system met with strong resistance from veteran appraisers who exercised considerable control over the real estate appraisal market.

They said that under the system using part-time appraisers, an appraisal report is made jointly by an appraisal company and an appraiser without employment relationship between them, which is not good. However, when a lot of appraisal requests came to trust banks, it was actually quite common that they subcontracted them to appraisers other than their own staff.

At meetings of real estate appraisal associations, these old-time appraisers were said to keep insisting the illegality of Sanyu's approach, but their assertions did not convince the land ministry and many other appraisers' will to work with us. The appraisers who took part in the system increased year after year. The opponents just had to argue for sentimental reasons and put themselves in a more difficult position.

During the last four or five years, organizations similar to Sanyu finally came into existence, and there is now much less pressure on Sanyu. For the last couple of years, the number of appraisers registered with us has rapidly increased.

The Tumult Over the "Efficient Appraisal Report"

As I wrote in chapter 5, in 1980 when Sanyu System was established, Japan Real Estate Appraisal Association devised a simplified appraisal form carrying only the minimum items needed for real estate appraisal. To appraise collateral for housing loan financing, the items laid down by the real estate appraisal law were sufficient and tens of pages of appraisal reports consisting mostly of long sentences were no longer considered necessary.

About that time, Sanyu System, whose clients were mainly banking institutions that offered housing loans, also came up with and commercialized its own simplified appraisal report forms. Since Sanyu System had monopolized marketing efforts to banking institutions those days, most of the appraisers who were doing appraisal work for banks were using our simplified forms. Shortly after that, I thought that the name "simplified appraisal form" might give our clients an impression that we are skimping our work. So I changed the term to "efficient appraisal report" and registered it as a trademark.

Subsequently, we visited banks with the idea of introducing the efficient appraisal report, and some banks bought it. But it was not customary to use appraisal reports in those days, and though some banks did understand the necessity of such reports, they still said our price 50 thousand yen was too high and asked if we had cheaper products.

Thus, we began to classify appraisal items by use so that clients could choose the least expensive product to meet their purposes, or what I term an "efficient real estate survey report." The efficient appraisal report was priced at 50 thousand yen because it was written by a qualified appraiser and the cost was higher accordingly. So, instead of appraisers, we made use of real-estate transaction specialists. We also took out of the form the items concerning "revenue" and "general factors" and included only the items needed by financial institutions. Thus, we pioneered the one-page report.

However, the real estate appraisal law prohibits people other than qualified appraisers from providing real estate appraisal values and receiving a fee for the service. Therefore, we decided to actually visit real estate agents in the area and ask them what they thought of a property or region in question. Then we included those findings by adding lines in the report noting that "at least two local agents" saw the price being such and such an amount.

We didn't call the efficient real estate survey report (the initial price was 15 thousand yen) appraisal report because it was simply a reference material not satisfying necessary requirements for the appraisal report, but it was good enough for actual business of banking institutions. The new product became a huge hit.

However, as products, the efficient real estate survey report and appraisal report met with unexpected trouble. At Sanyu System, "revenue" and "general factors" that are required to be included in appraisal reports and are appraisers' matters were thus not included in the survey reports. Some imprudent appraisers of other companies were submitting to banks as "efficient appraisal report" only the items included in the survey report of Sanyu; that is to say, reports that excluded the revenue and general factors material required of formal appraisals. (At Sanyu System, as a rule, efficient real estate survey reports were written by staff other than real estate appraisers.)

To be sure, efficient real estate appraisal reports were made by qualified appraisers, but what was written by our competitors did not meet the standard for real estate appraisal. It was simply a "survey report" and could not be called "appraisal report." Calling it an "appraisal report" meant they were selling it at a low survey fee. It was a fraudulent practice.

If it is an appraisal report made by an appraiser, 100 percent of the appraised value entered there will be recognized as the price of a property by Financial Services Agency, but if it is a survey report, only 70 percent of the price written there will be accepted even though it was written by an appraiser. As a result, if it is not recognized as an "appraisal report," the amount of bad debts will increase by 30 percent and it will be a big blow to financial institutions.

A problem occurred in about the year 2000 when the Financial Services Agency started investigating the bad loans of a bank which we had done business with. Seeing another company's "efficient real estate appraisal reports," the Agency notified the company that they were not real estate appraisal reports judging from the items written there.

Since the name of the report form was the same, the Agency did not recognize the efficient appraisal reports of Sanyu System either, causing trouble between the government agency and the banking institution. The bank hastily contacted us. It was only then that we learned such "appraisal reports"—what Sanyu System considers as cheaper survey reports by non-real estate appraisers—were in circulation among banking institutions.

If the government agency had checked the contents of our efficient appraisal reports, these kinds of problems would never have surfaced for us. It would be a real pain in the neck if trouble occurred every time a bank was inspected by the Agency. So, we had to change our trade names, "efficient appraisal report" and "efficient survey report" to "Sanyu standard form for real estate appraisal report" and "Sanyu standard survey report form." I wonder what name the firms that issued fake efficient appraisal reports are using now.

We all know that Xerox and Kleenex were originally the names of private companies that came to represent the products those companies made. Similarly, the name "efficient appraisal report" has almost become a common noun without our knowledge and has widely been misused in a way other than the usage of Sanyu. Fortunately, we found out about it an early stage and were able to keep the damage to a minimum. But the penalty in terms of harm to our reputation was indeed regretful. Even now, I feel nostalgic about the word "efficient."

Clients are selfish. A 15,000-yen survey report was still too expensive. I was asked by people from one life insurance company if we could come up with a cheaper product even at the cost of skipping visiting the property site. We are quite good at commercializing "selfishness." To be sure, if we are to evaluate a property which had been appraised less than a year ago, we can figure out its value at the desk. So we started selling handmade "Sanyu Desktop Assessment" for 10,000 yen. Jointly with TAS, we also developed. "TAS Map," which makes it possible to assess a property instantaneously on the computer. Now we are serving our clients with a unique line of products including "appraisal reports," "survey reports," "desktop assessments," and TAS Maps. Furthermore, joining up with a major real estate appraisal company of New York, Blake Inc., we are offering quick and inexpensive appraisal services in the United States.

Strong Opposition to Reasonable Fees

Just as in the case of the "part-time real estate appraiser system," the lowering of appraisal fees by the "efficient appraisal report" also caused a firestorm among existing appraisers. The fee structure that had been in practice was such that the higher the appraised value of a property was, the more fees appraisers could get, because appraisers receive a certain percentage of the appraised value. This fee structure had nothing to do with the level of difficulty of appraisal work. I just could not accept the payment structure, particularly in the case of appraising residential houses, since the fee difference could really be considerable. Suppose we evaluated two of the same houses; one in Denechoufu (something like the Beverly Hills of Japan) and the other in the suburban working class city of Machida. Because of the difference in unit price, the one in Denechoufu could be five to ten times more than that in Machida.

Whether the property is in Denechoufu or Machida, there is no difference in time and cost needed for appraising the properties. Depending on the location of a property, the appraisal fee could be as much or two or three times more expensive.

We can hardly convince the banking institutions that asked us to do the job. Since they have their own budget, it would also be hugely inconvenient for them if they did not know how much an appraisal would cost them until the value of the property had been determined.

For a residential house, the price of our efficient appraisal report was, regardless of where it was, 50,000 yen (when this service was first made available). It was one-fifth to one-tenth of the conventional prices. It was no wonder that a great shock hit veteran appraisers who had been enjoying comfortable fees under the fixed-percentage-rate remuneration scheme.

Sanyu System is a price-slashing firm. This was made possible thanks to the part-time appraisers system and the standardization and simplification of appraisal forms. Even though fees are low, Sanyu and each part-time appraiser make an agreement for each appraisal case and their compensation is on piecework. Under the system, part-time appraisers could receive each order on a profitable basis. Sanyu is also making profit though not as big as other old-time appraisal firms. Even though it might look like price slashing, it was absolutely a reasonable price setting.

Still, we were a lot more reasonable in price than other appraisal firms, and banks came to place large orders with us. Moreover, they gave us the work that used to be done by themselves. Sanyu created new demand.

When a newcomer in an industry dares to drive prices down, they usually get scolded by the government. However, the land ministry that was our supervisory authority at the time did not even show a sign of it, which puzzles us even today.

The head wind that we experienced from our peers started turning into a tail wind.

Fair Trade Commission

In the first half of the 1980s, a few years after the establishment of our company, a local municipal government on the northernmost big island of Hokkaido sought competing bids from local appraisers for the appraisal of a property it owned.

The bid was won by a young real estate appraiser at a considerably low price. The local appraisal industry was furious. A representative of Hokkaido Real Estate Association complained to the local government that it was not in line with the standard price of the industry.

The action of making a job open for bidding itself was commendable in those days. An official of the local government in charge suspected that the price cartel could be a violation of antitrust law and reported the case to the Fair Trade Commission. The investigation by the FTC made the Japan Real Estate Appraisal Association in Tokyo look like an upturned anthill.

Since then, real estate appraisal associations of the country have been extremely sensitive about cartel movements.

After the incident, there was a delicate change in the relationship between Sanyu System and real estate appraisal associations. Apparently they wanted to say that appraisal associations had not attempted or even allowed to guide appraisers to follow the standard prices. The fact that firms like Sanyu System, noted for a low prices, was a member of the association explains that.

Sanyu System has not changed a bit, but thanks to the change of surroundings, the enemies in the rest of the real estate appraisal industry became friends.

Clients, however, have always patronized us and we couldn't care less about the head wind in the industry.

Being in a Minority of One at the Time of Founding

As has been explained, Sanyu System was completely isolated soon after its founding. Naturally, there were not many who were willing to serve as part-time appraisers. Even if some were willing, they were new appraisers or new assistant appraisers who did not have jobs. They did not want their local appraisal association and fellow appraisers to know that they were working for Sanyu System and they kept it secret.

It seems that some appraisers who were found out to be working with Sanyu were threatened to be expelled from the association.

At present, approximately a fifth of more than 6,000 appraisers in Japan, that is to say 400 appraisers, are cooperating appraisers of Sanyu System. (The original name, part-time appraisers, was later changed to "affiliate appraisers" and at present "cooperating appraisers".) It is hard to believe, from our experience in the past, that some officers of local real estate appraisal associations are now our cooperating appraisers. It is said that by becoming Sanyu System's cooperating appraisers, local appraisers can have the firsthand knowledge and information of appraisal work in big cities. These cooperating appraisers are very important assets of Sanyu. To express that appreciation in a concrete way, we have taken out regular accident insurance, if they so desire, in the names of appraisers or their assistants and surveyors, for 5 million yen.

A Fresh Breeze for the Real Estate Appraisal Industry

When I entered into this business in around 1980, as mentioned in chapter 5, I was surprised to learn that those who passed the 2nd test of the real estate appraisal examination were going through apprenticeship and working at an appraisal office for little or no pay. From that experience, when Sanyu System employed those who passed the 2nd test, we always paid full salaries and actively promoted assistant appraisers as cooperating assistant appraisers.

Because of that, old-time appraisers who used to use successful candidates for the 2nd test for almost no pay had to increase the amount they paid their staff to hang on to them, resulting in the increase of office expenses for our competitors. Also, when their apprentices became independent as our cooperating appraisers, some offices were short-handed and could not even do on-the-spot surveys. Some of them also could not write appraisal reports without apprentices.

In order to keep apprentice appraisers, teacher-appraisers had to raise their pay, meaning increased personnel cost. Profits at our competitors suffered and unfinished work piled up. Veteran appraisers began to carry a grudge against me.

An amateur company, Sanyu System, coming in from a different industry, placed a lot of burden on existing real estate appraisers who at the time were enjoying a stable position in the appraisal business.

Their animosity was fierce.

In the summer of 2000, in appreciation of their cooperation for our work, we thought of donating several million yen each to Meikai University, Aoyama Gakuin University, the Japan Real Estate Appraisal Association, and the Japan Association for Real Estate Sciences in order for them to purchase books they needed.

However, at the Japan Real Estate Appraisal Association, the secretary general at that time strongly opposed accepting the donation and we had to give up the idea. I don't know if the opposition was his own sentiment or the judgment of the chairman of the association or the consensus of the entire board members. But there was a reason for the way old-time appraisers hated us. Veteran appraisers' patron clients were public organizations and Sanyu System never got into this field. If we had violated their turf even a little, it would have been much worse.

Now we don't have much dissension with old-time appraisers. It may be that they don't have as much say as they used to, or they gave up as a trend of times. Dissension, however, has not disappeared totally. Once a year or so, we get harassment from unexpected persons about any old unexpected matter. We try to think of it as having something akin to a traffic accident.

When a new accounting system for impaired assets is introduced in March 2006, if a book value (a figure on the balance sheet) of a property owned by a corporation becomes lower than the going price (market price), the difference (unrealized loss) must be written off. There will be new needs for the real estate appraisal market. In fact, we have already been asked by some ten firms to handle this problem.

While a decline of appraisal requests relating to bad loans is envisaged in the appraisal market, it can be expected that the accounting for impaired assets will create a stable demand. The number of business organizations that could be clients for the coming need to account for impaired assets is incomparably bigger than that of financial institutions and the work continues year after year. While the jobs that come from financial institutions concentrate in the latter half of fiscal year as appraisal reports must be the ones that were made within six months from the end of the fiscal year, the work related to the impaired assets accounting is dispersed more or less evenly throughout the year.

In recent years, young appraisers who are well-versed in such a new market and its peripheral businesses are now emerging, and the industry will soon be led by those next generation appraisers.

The outdated characteristics of the industry will also change in a matter of a short period.

Different Roles of Appraisal Firms and Appraisers

The part-time system explained before made it possible for appraisers to work for other firms than the appraisal firm they belong to and consequently appraisal companies and appraisers were separated. This meant that Sanyu System didn't have to just concentrate on sales work. My way of living is not to attempt too much and not to go too fast and this motto has reflected on Sanyu System's way of doing business. If we ask a bank to give us some appraisal work to do, we cannot ignore their request for the value they like. If we make hard sales, it will come back to us with tough requirements. Who knows what might be asked, such as, "In secret we want this particular item to be appraised double the appropriate price."

Sanyu System ignores requests (meaning direction) for appraised value from clients. Even if we are asked, we answer positively on the spot, but we do not convey any conditions to our appraisers. The relation between the sales company and a part-time appraiser is that between an ordering party and an order receiving party, but we cannot take advantage of the position as an ordering party and exert pressure on part-time appraisers.

It may be primarily that such types of business as banking institutions, credit guarantee companies, financing companies, real estate appraisal companies, CPAs, and tax accountants whose interest often conflicts with that of clients and who sometimes has to make decisions against the client's desire should not be sales oriented. However, an appraisal company like Sanyu System cannot help being engaged in selling. Balancing is difficult.

This is a trap small appraisal firms can easily fall into. We often witness tragedies resulting from their hard sales. Some had their licenses suspended. We must have courage to stop dealing with firms that ask too much about appraised values.

Sanyu System does not accept any joining fees and annual dues from cooperating appraisers, because should we receive them, they may complain for more work and we may have to sell hard to banking institutions to accommodate them.

We must avoid creating problems for the future that might be caused by increasing the number of cooperating appraisers for more annual fees, engaging in hard sales for more appraisal work, receiving unreasonable requests from clients, asking appraisers to come up with unreasonable appraisal values, and sending absurd appraisal reports to the world.

Real Estate Appraisers Having Artisan Spirit

Real estate appraisers have their own artisan spirit. Putting their whole self into creating something excellent is a good aspect of artisans. Sometimes, however, that is the only thing in their mind and they tend to pay little or no attention to how long it takes or how much it costs. They stick to "something good" and often cannot accommodate all of their clients' intentions or cannot just swim with the flow.

In the summer of 2004, I went to Koriyama in Fukushima Prefecture on business. There I met a noted figure in the appraisal industry, Mr. Shinichi Hashimoto, and exchanged views on how appraisal companies and appraisers should be in the future. Mr. Hashimoto introduced an episode for us to ponder.

"An appraiser I know was asked by a certain tax accountant to appraise a property owned by an individual. If the appraised value is lower than the assessment of the tax office, the tax will be 200 thousand yen less. Since it would still be to his benefit even if he paid 100 thousand yen, he wanted the appraisal fee to be 100 thousand yen. To this, the appraiser said 'No,' saying the amount of saving in tax has nothing to do with his appraisal fee and that he would not accept the work unless he is paid 250 thousand yen for the appraisal work. What do you think of that?"

It is an interesting example. One way of answering it will be to say, "I always make my appraisal report using the same method and therefore it will cost you 250 thousand yen." Another way will be to give a discount of 100 thousand yen now that the order is there.

Or, a more business-minded appraiser might choose to make an appraisal report for 100 thousand yen by lawfully simplifying it. I feel that many newly qualified appraisers will choose this third way.

Surely there are enterprising appraisers with excellent senses of business.

If I may give my candid opinion, there are many veteran appraisers who, in addition to being artisans, do not want others to encroach upon their territory and protect their vested interests to maintain the level of incoming orders. Naturally, those people do not want people of new thinking to come in. At the same time they do not want to enter a new business either. Professionally, they are conservatives. They never even think how much they are contributing to society with their work. The older they are, the stronger this tendency seems.

When we think of appraisers' technical knowledge and ability, they should enter into fields where they can make more contributions to society, and I think they are capable of doing so. Even within the framework of real estate appraisal business, other than doing accurate appraisal work, I think it is possible to do the work faster and at less cost. There is also room for developing new products that meet the nationwide (or preferably international) needs of clients.

A New Market Called Due Diligence

In the year 2004, such leading companies as Kanebo, Daiei, and my old place of work, Misawa, asked the quasi-governmental Industrial Revitalization Corporation of Japan for its management assistance. Tactics between the corporation, the companies in question and their main banks, were reported almost every day on the mass media.

The topic almost always talked about in the news was "due diligence," that is to say, asset assessment. This practice is new to Japan.

Without knowing the value of the assets held by a company to be assisted, nobody will know in what area the assistance should be given and to what extent. Due diligence is an indispensable task for revitalizing a company.

Due diligence is a coined term spotlighted when U.S. real estate companies and banking institutions set up operations in Japan from 1995 to 2000. It was a Western way of evaluation introduced by American financial funds that began a bulk purchase of bad loans in this country.

Due diligence originally referred to the work involved in a company buyout; checking out and evaluating the financial standing and technical capabilities of the company to be bought out, but in the world of real estate, it is also used for real estate transactions for investment purposes as well as for project financing. It is sometimes called "fair evaluation procedure" to figure out appropriate market value of a property to be transacted as well as the risks involved.

For due diligence, it is necessary to analyze the physical condition (such as location) of a target property as well as the price and rent market, and to check out the rights or presence of lawsuits etc., all of which are what real estate appraisers are always dealing with. Analyzing price and the rental market, as well as location, are what appraisers are good at.

However, I don't often hear that real estate appraisers are positively accepting requests for due diligence. Neither have I heard that the Japan Real Estate Appraisal Association held workshops on due diligence for its members. At best, prefectural associations are holding workshops sporadically.

I think due diligence has some good prospects. Nevertheless, the Japan Real Estate Appraisal Association would not consider due diligence as a kind of real estate appraisal and has not actively developed new products for it. They have not done anything about lawyers and accountants selling good products in the field of due diligence. I often utter a sigh of grief how real estate appraisers lack an enterprising spirit. The real estate appraisal business has so many business interfaces; real property management, realty, construction, finance, judicial scrivener, land surveyors, registered land and building investigators, architects, soil contamination surveyors, etc. Despite the fact that there are unlimited industries related to real estate appraisal business, hardly anybody attempts to enter into other fields for job possibilities or for jointly developing new products.

The Bad Traditions of the Real Estate Appraisal Industry

Seen from the eyes of a newcomer like me, there is a kind of tradition in the appraisal industry that I find so difficult to comprehend. It relates to the domination of the industry by old-time appraiser, which I mentioned before.

For one thing, depending on the year appraisers obtained a qualification, a hierarchical relation is brought about automatically. All societies or communities have their juniors and seniors. It is a natural phenomenon and there is nothing wrong with that. But in the real estate appraisal industry, its hierarchical relation seems to be hampering the development of the industry.

In the real estate appraisal industry, there are two types of firms: "companies centering on sales" trying to obtain orders for appraisal work and "real estate appraisal report making companies" contracting to do appraisal work and produce reports. When a sales company asks a production company to make an appraisal report, if the president of the sales firm happens to be a junior to that of a production company, the latter sometimes will not accept the request. He doesn't want to be beneath the dignity receiving an order from his junior.

Other than the strange hierarchical relation, in our industry there has been a misconception that one that gives an order is superior to one that accepts it. It is for that reason that some outsourcing sales companies are finding it difficult to improve their businesses.

Sanyu System is pretty much an outsourcing-type sales company. The reason that we have been able to grow at least could be that I don't have a qualification as an appraiser and have been outside the hierarchical relationship of the real estate appraisal industry.

There is another custom that I am concerned about. That is the struggle between real estate appraisal firms registered with the minister whose main line of business is banking or real estate and those registered with the governor.

Banks and real estate companies registered with the minister for real estate appraisal business are well-known throughout the country with strong brand power and are quite influential in the economic world, but top executives of those companies do not have qualifications as real estate appraisers in most cases. Naturally, they have little knowledge about real estate appraisal and have little time to think about the real estate appraisal industry seriously.

On the other hand, those registered with the governor are totally unknown outside the appraisal industry and their annual sales will be 20 or 30 million yen at best. As business persons, they are mavericks and often self-centered.

However, the number of appraisers who work for firms registered with the governor is four times those working for firms registered with the minister. Besides, a majority of appraisers working for big companies registered with the minister are very independent-minded since they chose to be appraisers because they did not want to end up their lives as merely salaried persons. When they do become independent, they can never be a big scale appraisal company registered with the minister from the beginning. They have no choice but to start as a small appraisal firm registered with the governor. Thus, the difference in number of appraisers between companies registered with the minister and those registered with the governor is expected to widen in the future.

In terms of such sales aspects as publicity, processing capability, and territorial magnitude, appraisal firms registered with the minister overwhelm those registered with the governor, but in terms of the number of appraisers, the reverse is the case. Their interests often interfere with each other and their confrontation often gets fierce. The hostility was brought to light at the time of electing the chairperson at the Japan Real Estate Appraisal Association.

Until 2003, the chairperson's seat of the Japan Real Estate Appraisal Association, which is the headquarters of local appraisal associations, was held by representatives of big companies. Just to name the last few: Mr. Hideo Matsuo of Tokyu Real Estate, Mr. Seiichi Kawasaki of former Mitsui Trust Bank, and Mr. Tetsuo Aki of Tokyu Real Estate assumed the position. They are either presidents or ex-presidents of big companies. At an early stage of the appraisal industry, it was necessary for a representative of a reputable established company to assume the post of chair.

However, as the number of firms registered with the governor grew, they began to have a desire to send a person representing their interests to the post of chair. At the election held in 2004, Mr. Hiroshi Yokosuka of the Yokosuka Real Estate Appraisal Office, a company registered with the governor, was chosen as the first chairperson from the governor's group. Now that the representative of the majority group has become the chairperson, it is expected that he will be active enough to come up with his new policy for the industry.

But the truth of the matter is that the conflict between big companies and medium- and small-sized appraisal companies is almost at the boiling point. In the near future, they may break up into two trade organizations.

Real estate appraisers are legally protected, qualified specialists. Since they have no problem in supporting themselves, they are conscious of being independent. They put considerable energy into maintaining their independence and, therefore, it should be extremely difficult for the entire industry to come together as one. Unless, however, they join together for developing new fields, it is obvious the work that is supposed to be done by appraisers might be eaten away by other industries and the appraisal industry itself might dry up. I cannot help but be concerned about it.

Conclusion

On January 19, 2005, in his scheduled briefing for reporters, Governor Toshihiko Fukui of the Bank of Japan was asked what he thought about the rise in real estate transaction prices that had been noted in some quarters. Mr. Fukui expressed his perception that the prices of land in central Tokyo in particular were beginning to rise to a certain extent. He added that they should watch very carefully whether price movements, particularly upward movements, were excessive or not.

Mr. Fukui's perception itself is correct, but actually things are moving in the opposite direction.

Since the days of the bubble, I have kept saying that land prices of Japan would drop by half. My thoughts have not changed until now, in 2005, when I am finishing up this book. The reason for saying that was given in this book and I think the drop in land prices is a phenomenon in the waves of a short-term fluctuation of the economy after the burst of the bubble. The current economic situation is a result of the short-term fluctuation plus the waves of big economic changes brought about by declining population.

Long-time decrease in population and the number of families coupled with the decline in land prices will result in the reintegration of residential lots.

Whether through a land taxation system or through environment policy, I want the government to pre-empt the change in ownership structure of land and its utilization caused by the population decrease. One example could be to remit their real property acquisition tax and fixed property tax when people move to a more spacious lot or build a house on a lot integrating that of a next door neighbor's that they purchased.

There are some people in the economic world who hold concerns that the total economic output might drop as a result of the population decrease, but shouldn't we also see the aspect that despite a drop in the total gross domestic product, if the GDP per person increases, we can have a better natural and living environment? I personally support a population decrease on a global scale.

As of 2004, the world population is 6 billion 400 million. It is predicted that it will be 9 billion 300 million in the year 2050 (according to Population Reference Bureau, a population research group). It is also pointed out that sooner or later a great number of people will die of hunger resulting from food shortage.

While in Europe, worried about the decrease in population, some countries are seeking to encourage population growth through subsidies. In China they have promoted the one-child policy by law. In Japan, the population is declining naturally. I may say, Japan is an honor student of the earth community. I don't trust people who support principles but cave on particulars, like some intellects who express concern about the world population increase on one hand and complain about the declining population of Japan on the other.

If the world population declines to the level of 200 years ago, food insecurity and global warming will be solved, and as we consume less electricity, we can do away with troublesome generation facilities and worsening global environment will improve.

Though I talked big, we, Sanyu System Appraisal, have managed to survive in the current trend of economy and society. It was fortunate that I could write my first book in the year 2005 when Sanyu System celebrated its 25th Anniversary.

Looking back upon the past, I think I have managed the company like scooping millet with wet hands (a Japanese saying meaning "make easy gain"). To other people it might have looked as if I was raking in profits, but it is not that I have done something sly or that I have been lucky.

In order to scoop as much grain as possible, you have to know where a big pile of grain is. Even if you found some piles, you would have to compare them to know which pile is tasty and harmless, which is a better pile, or which to try first. Now that you have good piles of grain, you have to think about how you wet your hands. Since the purpose of getting millet grain is for food, you cannot put coal tar on your hands. Grain scooped with those hands cannot even be cattle feed.

Hands wet with water, however, will not get more grain than hands with tar. You have to eat less grain.

With what kind of water you wet your hands is another question. You can wet your hands with ice or with steam. Warm water will also do.

Even when putting your wet hands into a pile of millet grain, if you wait too long and your hands get dry, you cannot scoop a lot of grain.

If you want to make easy gains, you must seek and find that opportunity. Everyone has the same objective of obtaining millet, but to accomplish the end, you must always think of when, where, and how you do it before other people. It is not easy to do that every day. Needless to say, you must be careful not to get foam—which is called "*awa*" in Japanese—instead of millet—which is also called "*awa*".

This book may also be a result of my way of scooping millet with wet hands.

I really owe a lot to many people for publishing this book.

I must buy drinks for Mr. Katsuaki Tsuneyoshi and Mr. Haruki Yoshida who gave me a lot of advice regarding the contents of the book. Many thanks also go to Mr. Soichiro Mori who helped reconstruct my amateurish manuscript, did some supplementary research, and rewrote my writing. I am also thankful to

Naoko Inoue, second daughter of my deceased brother, Teruyoshi Inoue, for spending a lot of time on this book.

Sanyu System Real Estate and Finance Institute has been conducting its unique surveys, the results of which had added some depth to this book. Without complaint, the person in charge, Mr. Hideo Hirose, did questionnaire surveys and other analysis work that just came to my mind.

I would also like to thank Mr. Shin Matsuura, a reporter of *Asahi Shimbun* (editorial staff of *Be*) and an old friend of mine who was instrumental in publishing this book. To Ms. Naomi Akaiwa, also of *Asahi* in charge of book editorial, I must bow my head deep.

One of my friends who is a newspaper reporter said to me, "Once you write a book, you will want to write a second and a third." I said to him, "I'm out of material. I don't feel like writing anymore."

We'll see.

Postscript: Is Real Estate in the State of Mini-Bubble Now?

June 7, 2007
At Yamanote Rotary Club Meeting in Tokyo
Akiyoshi Inoue

1. The History of Postwar Real Estate Bubbles

The period from the launching of what was called "the Japanese archipelago remodeling plan" to its tumbling is the first postwar bubble. At that time, prices fell after its peak in 1974, but the price fall was seen only in 1975 and it started to rise again from 1976. This virtually endorsed the myth of ever-higher land prices. People in those days would say, "Even if prices fall, just put up with it for a couple of years and they will go up again."

As you might recall, the first period was characterized by hard sales on the part of real estate firms. Since money was tight, banking institutions could be selective in offering loans. Although many real estate companies went bankrupt, banks did not have to suffer from bad debts.

The second period saw the birth of bubble and the burst of bubble. It started in 1986–87, reached its peak in '88 and after a few years of leveling off, prices continued to fall for more than ten years. This period coincides with that of worldwide easing of money after the Plaza Accord in September 1985, and Japanese banking institutions were struggling for finding ways to operate their funds.

Because of this, real estate investment was no longer the monopoly of land agents. I might say it was banking institutions that took the lead. Calling it "good-office business," they referred properties to real estate agents with necessary funds. Not only that, they even exerted pressure on appraisal companies to appraise properties at higher prices so that they can offer higher amount of loans.

Banking institutions were not interested in considering whether supply matches demand but in offering more loans.

Being engaged in the appraisal business, I must be concerned with the social influence of our work, for the price of real estate next to the property appraised by us is often affected by our price. I strongly felt it not right that the price of land be determined not by supply and demand but by the list prices of banking institutions. I was very much concerned that unlike the first period of bubble, there could be some banking institutions that would crash. My anxiety proved correct.

The second price hike was seen nationwide, from northernmost Hokkaido to southernmost Okinawa, from big cities to small rural towns. The decisive difference between the first and second periods was the fact that banking institutions were involved in the fall of the bubble in the second period. It was only a decade ago that many big city banks and such urban non-banks as housing loan or leasing companies, as well as insurance firms, failed in big cities where the land bubble was particularly intensive and extensive.

A considerable number of foreign banks and funds also joined the show but unlike exaggerated news coverage when they came in, those that failed quietly left the stage.

2. Is the Current Rise in Land Prices a Bubble?

Should we call the current state of land prices a bubble or is it just a natural phenomenon? The price rise of land we see now was not caused by an increase in demand. We are in easy money times, and as was the case before, office buildings and condominiums have been supplied at the initiative of banking institutions. Particularly, loaning on real-estate related businesses by urban banking institutions accounts for a high percentage. We will have to call it the third bubble.

Then what is the difference between the previous bubbles and the current bubble? What is different this time is that the areas where land prices have gone up are limited to the metropolis, or rather parts of the metropolis.

One thing that is different is the behavior of banking institutions. Having learned a lesson, mega-banks are not enthusiastic about real-estate loaning with the exception of certain housing loans. Non-banks have either failed or have been weakened. Consequently they are not very active.

What entered the market in their stead are newly commercialized investment funds involving real estate.

The funds that went public on the Tokyo and other stock exchanges aiming at minor investors among the general public are commonly called J-REIT. Those that are not listed are classified as "privately placed bonds."

Since the yield of J-REIT is higher than other deposit interests or financial products, individual investors are purchasing it, and it is said that instead of investing on real estate directly, foreign capitals are also purchasing it in large quantities.

Privately placed bonds are not listed and their information is not made available to the general public, making it difficult to know their real picture. Those who purchase this product are such banking institutions as local banks, credit associations, and credit cooperatives that are not as sound as city banks and are finding it difficult to manage their funds.

The real estate investment trust is a product that came into being only five or six years ago, and because of its short history they found it necessary to purchase properties quickly so that they can start business with zero assets. That often forced them to ask appraisers to evaluate the property at higher prices although they were aware that it is not the way.

It cannot be denied that the conduct of investment trust traders are partially responsible for the real estate price hike because they have to buy properties at higher prices even knowing that it is not right.

I think there are three elements that cause a bubble to collapse. One is when the balance of supply and demand is destroyed. At present, companies are doing better than expected, so it will not be difficult to find tenants for newly constructed office buildings. But personal income has not increased so much. An expensive high-rise condominium crash might ignite a bubble burst.

Location-wise, condominiums adjacent to areas where land prices violently went up could be left unsold or become less expensive.

Another element is when the Bank of Japan raises its policy rate following the world-wide trend for higher interest rates. The reason that REIT is selling is because its yield is better than deposit interests and national bonds. Once the bank rate goes up, REIT prices will go down rapidly, which will lead to mass selling of REIT by investors. As a consequence, REIT traders will find it difficult to organize new REIT and even for the REIT already drawn up, refinancing of their loans will not be easy. They will be forced to sell the property involved in the REIT. This will invite the lowering of land prices.

The third element is the movement of foreign funds that have invested in Japan's real estate. If better real estate items are available in other countries, or when economic environment changes as a result of Japan's high interest rate policy, they will be quicker than you can imagine at running away.

Let us think what effects will be brought about as a result of the decline in price. In the case of the previous bubble, major banks did receive damages, but depositors did not have to suffer thanks to the deposit insurance adopted by their banks. This time, however, investors will be directly affected by the fall of property prices, since investment trust is to be operated at investors' own risks and the government assumes no responsibility whatsoever.

Since local banks, credit associations, and credit cooperatives are prestigious members of that locality and as far as we can see from Tokyo, their outstanding deposits are relatively small, and even if they failed, its effect on banking institutions seems to be limited. But to depositors and loan customers in the area, the influence should be as great as that on major banks in the metropolis.

Since there are many local banks, credit associations, and credit cooperatives, their bailout will not be easy although the amount of money involved may be insignificant. People are concerned about widening economic gaps among regions these days, so caution must be taken not to invite credit uncertainty in those regions.

3. The Long-Range Prospect of Land Prices

Until recently all we had to think about property prices for the future was for five or at the longest ten to twenty years. But since the real estate investment trust made its debut, short-term predictions came to be required just as in stock investment. Sometimes we must predict the price of a property for tomorrow.

Sixty years have passed since the end of the last war. Here, I would like to attempt predicting how land will be used sixty years from now and what the prices of land will be then.

After the last war, the population of Japan increased and the country switched from an agricultural to an industrial nation. Accordingly, the pattern of using land, which used to be forestation and farming, changed to industrial and residential. This resulted in the rise in price of the industrial land as compared with that of farmland. Prices of land for factories and houses in our near big cities, and that for commercial and office buildings, have skyrocketed beyond imagination.

Wooded areas and farmland near a city are favorably appraised if they are recognized as "prospective residential land."

Reviewing the past fifty or more years after the last war, we might find ourselves standing at a very important and crucial turning point as seen in such structural changes as the change in the use of land and the price of land. First, there is a population decline. Suppose two families are living next to each other in a 50-*tsubo* (a Japanese unit of measuring land space that is still used commonly: 1 tsubo = 3.3 square meters) house in a suburban area. One family has a son and the other a daughter. They get married. One house is now in excess. Thus, the suburban land becomes idle and desolate. The land would be turned into "prospective farmland" such as a kitchen garden, orchard, or wooded area and eventually into genuine farmland.

As the first structure changes, the use of land will change greatly and as a consequence there will be less residential land and more farmland.

In the meantime, prices of agricultural products are rising for unexpected reasons. Corn, barley, and other vegetables have come to be used for alternative energy. Prices of strategic agricultural products will reflect this phenomenon and be raised over a period of time. Naturally, other farm products will become higher in price also.

As for Japan, such products as rice, vegetables, and fruit will be exported at higher prices as pesticide-free quality products.

So the second point is that while industrial products will be less expensive due to mass production, agricultural products will be more expensive.

Thirdly, the prices of farmland that produce more expensive agricultural products will naturally be pushed up. This leads us to assume that the ratio between urban land prices, which constantly surpassed farmland prices in postwar years, and prices of farmland may be, if not reversed, narrowed considerably.

The total areas of land in Japan that have been neglected and left unused amount to the size of the Saitama Prefecture. This will work as a cushion, so I am not saying that residential land will soon be cultivated into farmland or the price of farmland will go up in a few years.

The question is what measures the agricultural ministry and the land ministry are going to take to cope with the structural changes I have mentioned. The government is trying to work mainly on the service-based economy. For example, they are trying to match their monetary policy to the international standard. I think the government should first work out a policy that will revolutionize Japan's agriculture, which inevitably will go through structural changes in the near future.

Japan will then shift from an industrial and technological nation to a country of two pillars: industry and agriculture.